My Kind of Town

150 years of Bridport's news

by Margery Hookings

© Margery Hookings 2005

Printed by
Creeds the Printers
Broadoak
Bridport
Dorset
DT6 5NL

Published by
Margery Hookings
King Charles Cottage
The Square
Broadwindsor
Beaminster
Dorset
DT8 3QD

ISBN-10: 0-9551925-0-1

ISBN-13: 978-0-9551925-0-0

Foreword	7
How it all began	8
The first year	11
The workhouse	14
The town hall and pavements	15
Who was Boneshaker?	16
A sporting tradition	17
The railway	18
Memories of 100 years ago	20
Saturday night at the movies	34
Memories of 50 years ago	36
Firewater to cure all ills	39
By Royal appointment	40
Peter and Mary Payne	42
Wimpy bars and platform soles	44
Bowling them over	46
From punk to editor	48
Find Fido	51
From marketing to reporting	52
A man made in Bridport	54
The aim remains the same	55

HOME SWEET HOME: The Bridport and Lyme Regis News office in East Street (BN)

FOREWORD

THE BRIDPORT News celebrated its 150th anniversary in the year 2005.

The newspaper began as the Crimean war was coming to an end.

It has reported the comings and goings of this small country town and surrounding area for the last century-and-a-half.

This book is not meant to be the definitive history of a weekly paper referred to by locals as the 'Wip Wop'.

The supplement that came out with the News on June 24, 2005, tells that story more than adequately.

But I hope it conveys something of the flavour of Bridport and its inhabitants, how things have changed and yet stayed very much the same.

Reading through the old copies of the News – on microfilm at Bridport Library – you get a real sense of time and place. The language and detail in those early years is quite astonishing. Like everywhere else, Bridport has witnessed many changes in the last 150 years.

It has seen the arrival of the industrial age, the railway, the motor car, the telephone, television and cinema.

Today, the internet rules the roost.

But despite that, the same old themes recur week after week, month after month and year after year.

Even 150 years ago, people were complaining about the state of the pavements. And if you look at Bridport Museum's old pictures, the townscape hasn't really altered very much.

Those wide streets, the Georgian buildings and the four faces of the Town Hall clock dominating the street scene from all directions.

A couple of years ago, I received a surprise visit from a man called Arthur Townsend, who was a reporter for the News in the 1950s.

He emigrated to Australia but had a strong affection for Bridport – and the News – not least because it was the town where he met his late wife.

As he sat down and talked to me and Terry Collin, the News's late sports editor, I said to Arthur: "You must write this down."

Not long after, he sent me an e-mail from the other side of the world, telling the story of a young man who joined a well-established newspaper and how it left a lasting impression on him.

My only regret is that Terry died before he was able to contribute – the stories he had about the area, many of which he'd gleaned from his late, great predecessor Roger Bailey, were amazing.

This book is dedicated to Terry and Roger.

Margery Hookings
Bridport News Editor 1999-2004

Bridport news

Once upon a time in the west

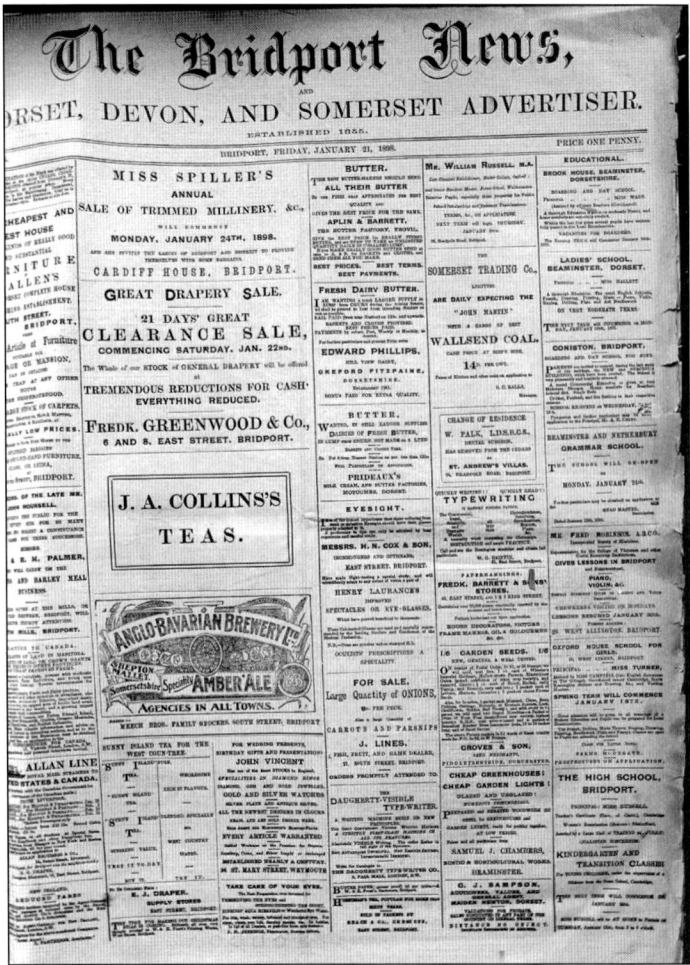

ABOVE AND BELOW: The Bridport News in its early days packed with advertisements on the front pages

THE first edition of the Bridport News rolled off a Colombian handpress on June 23, 1855, at William Charles Frost's little printing office in East Street, Bridport, next to the Unitarian Chapel.

The paper cost a penny. News from the battlefront of the Crimean War, together with artists' steel engravings, occupied more than half its columns.

In 1855, the branch railway line to Maiden Newton (now defunct) was just about to be built.

There were no telephones, cars or aeroplanes and most printing was still done by hand.

JUNE 28 1856
IT was reported that the switch from the illustrated version of the news to the one containing local, national and international news had been favourably received.

"We shall be glad to receive and insert articles, intelligence and correspondence, on matters of local interest, and may safely promise that our columns shall be 'open to all parties and influenced by none.'...

"Free from the shackles of political bias – it circulates in every circle, and amongst all parties in this town, and also at Lyme, Charmouth and in all the surrounding villages."

Circulation was 700-750 and the proprietors were aiming to hit the 1,000 mark.

Mr Frost set up his printing business in 1847, eight years before launching the News.

It was a time when the local weekly newspaper in Britain was just coming into its own.

This was because the Newspaper Tax, which had meant fourpenny newspapers (you could buy a lot with 4d in those days) had been repealed.

Local news made the front page for the first time on July 11, 1855, in a report previewing the second exhibition of the Bridport Horticultural Society. A meeting of the shareholders of Bridport Railway Company heard that work had started and 'every hope might be entertained of the line being completed by the autumn of next year'.

There was a report about the annual tea meeting of the scholars and teachers in the Bridport Unitarian Sunday Schools. It had been hoped to hold it on Eype Down but thick fog and a downpour of rain forced them to use the school room instead.

Six months after the first Bridport News hit the streets, improvements were announced.

On December 29, it appeared as a broadsheet of four pages and dispensed with the engravings.

It wasn't long before advertisements took up the whole front page, a tradition that went on until the late 1940s.

In 1862, Mr Frost moved his business to West Street, where Frosts' shop still operates today.

The building used to be a chemist's shop run by Mr ES Knight before it became a stationer's and printing office.

Earliest deeds show that in 1786 it was the White Hart Inn and in later deeds is mentioned as the Antelope. William Frost built up a

IN THE PICTURE: West Street showing the Bridport News' office (BM)

Growing with the times

healthy newspaper business and retired in 1877.

He was succeeded by his sons, William and Charles, and when Charles died, William was joined by his sister Emily Frost in developing the business.

In 1907, William died suddenly and his widow ran the business for many years. His sister died in 1935, at the age of 85.

William's son, Wilfred, was in charge of the newspaper between the wars and among the many improvements he introduced was machine type-setting.

When he retired in 1948, the business was acquired by a group of local conservatives, which retained the Frost name and operated as Messrs W Frost and Company Limited.

Leslie Heber Bruce, a sub-editor on the Yorkshire Evening Post, was appointed editor and the board included former MP for West Dorset, Sir Philip Colfox and his successor, Simon Wingfield Digby, who represented the area from 1941 to 1974.

News replaced the advertisements on the front page and the Bridport News entered a new era. The West Street works was a hive of activity with the acquisition of other papers – the Dorset County Chronicle and the Southern Times.

These were all typeset and printed at the old Frosts' works.

In 1956, Heber Bruce returned to his old papers in Leeds.

The News became part of the Salisbury Journal series in 1957, with the printing works closing down five years later and moving to Salisbury.

In 1967, it was taken over by the Berrows organisation, moving into the Somerset County Gazette series and was printed at Taunton.

By 1980, it belonged to News

ABOVE: West Street in Bridport, circa 1900 (BM)
BELOW: Melville Square at around the same period (BM)

International and in latter years, it was part of Southern Newspapers, which was then taken over by Newscom and finally, Newsquest, the UK's second largest publisher of regional and local newspapers.

Editors included Leslie Grellis, David Patrick, Bill Harris, John Slater, David Cozens and Margery Hookings. In 2004, Holly Robinson, formerly chief reporter and news editor of the Wiltshire Times, became editor.

Stories from 1857-2005

OCTOBER 1857
ALLINGTON – On Thursday afternoon last, three children named Thomas and Ellen Walbridge and Anna Maria Clarke – all under thirteen years of age – entered by the window a cottage occupied by John Martin, a labourer, and stole a brush, a toy table, and a few other trifling articles. The occupiers of the cottage were absent at work at the time.

A neighbour had seen the children near the cottage and on the houses of their parents being searched the missing property was found.

They were taken before S Cox, Esq at Beaminster and were committed for trial at the sessions.

The poor little creatures are much neglected. Clarke has no mother and the Walbridges are fatherless, with a bedridden mother.

JANUARY 1858
MARRIAGE OF THE PRINCESS ROYAL: On Monday last, Bridport did not get beyond its usual demonstrations on occasions calling for public rejoicing. Nearly all the shops and banks were closed; the bells of St Mary's Church rung at intervals, and a flag on the market house and tower did what they could to denote that the occasion on which the business was partially suspended was a joyous one.

But the dreary weather and the absence of the more inspiring and joyous strains of the town band caused the day to appear very dull. There were no public balls, nor dinners. no demonstrations of trades, nor processes of children on schools followed by a treat of plum cake and tea, no illuminations nor attempt at illuminations.

AUGUST 1860
IN spite of the earnest protestations of 'eye witnesses', and the minute delineations of engravers, the sea serpent hitherto has been placed by the public in the same category as Barnum's woolly horse, and his mysterious mermaid.

Scepticism on the point, however, can no longer exist in the minds of the Bridport public, for we have the testimony of a gentleman well-known in the neigbourhood, as to the existence of the fabulous monster of the deep, and that, too, at but a very short distance from Bridport Harbour.

Capt Jarvis, of the Good Intent, of this port, states in a communication to his uncle residing in Harbour Road, which has been handed to us, that on Saturday, July 28, at about 4pm, when about three miles from Portland Bill, he saw on the port-bow a large fish … it was found to be the sea serpent amusing itself by lashing the water, with about 30 feet of its tail, just as a coachman flourishes a whip. Next was observed 'what appeared to be the monster's head, and part of its body, about the size of a beer barrel'. Its extreme length was considered to be not less than from 70-80 feet.

ABOVE: Bridport Fire Brigade, 1897 (BM)

RIGHT: Happy Island, a popular beauty spot (BM)

BELOW: West Allington in 1909 (BM)

The first year of the News

THE FIRST Bridport News hit the streets on Saturday, June 23, 1855. It promised to be a 'faithful chronicler of our local history', although the first edition had just two of its eight pages devoted to local events.
The following week, it was urging readers to use their votes wisely in elections. This did not apply to women, who did not get the right to vote in local elections until 1907 and only if they were ratepayers.
It was only in 1918 that women were allowed to vote in parliamentary elections.

JUNE 1855

FAR be it from us to accuse our townsmen as a body of active criminality but there is such a vice as criminal indifference and we are often compelled to remember the liberal, but truthful lines of Hood: 'but evil is wrought by want of thought as well as by want of heart'.

So it is especially with many of the Electors of this Town, and what we would draw their attention to, is the fact that the vote is almost a religious privilege, to be exercised with care and deliberation and an earnest desire to use it honestly and rightly, not for individual benefit solely but for the wealth and welfare of a country and a world, thus indirectly, but no less certainly, of the individual – that even the poorest amongst the electoral body should hold up his head with honest pride which should make him conscious of this right, endeavour with all his heart and soul now to misapply or abuse that power which it should be his greatest boast to preserve.

THE 'kind hearted lady' Florence Nightingale has fallen ill at her post in the Crimea. The Siege of Sebastopol goes on. The Queen visits the wounded heroes at Brompton Hospital.

SMUGGLING AT BRIDPORT HARBOUR
PETER Barrett, Dennis Brannan and Thomas Kenway were charged with having contraband tobacco on board the Smack, Melinda, from Jersey, of which they were masters and crew.

The prisoners were fined £100 each and in default of payment to be imprisoned for six months.

Being unable to pay the fine they were committed to Dorchester Gaol.

JULY

THE Crimea and developments in the Baltic and Spain were reported copiously, complete with etchings.

SHEEP STEALING
ON Wednesday night, some miscreants stole a ewe sheep from the fold of Mr Job Hansford, of Uploders, and severed the head.

We hope the perpetrators of this deed will speedily be captured and receive the punishment they deserve.

HARD LABOUR
ON Saturday the July 21, William Orchard was brought up before the Mayor T Legg Esq on a charge of neglecting to support his wife and family and was committed to hard labour at Dorchester Gaol for one month.

IMMEDIATE POSSESSION
A convenient cottage situate at Wanderwell containing two bedrooms and two rooms under
Rent, £6 per annum
for further particulars, apply to Mr Frost, Bookseller, Bridport.

AUGUST

BRIDPORT CEMETERY
THE works of the new cemetery in the East Road have now been commenced, upwards of 20 men being employed in excavating and leveling, and by today it is very likely the new road will have been cut through to the turnpike.

BRIDPORT TEETOTAL SOCIETY
A MEETING took place of the above society at the Town Hall on Thursday evening, the attendance was considerable, more especially of the working classes.

PEA STEALING
JULIA Garland, Mary Diment and Mary Morris received a summons

PLEASE TURN TO PAGE 12

ADVERT

PRIME CIDER

for sale in Bridport Harbour

Richard Pinney begs to announce that he has just been advised of the shipment of a quantity of

PRIME JERSEY CIDER

which will arrive in a day or two. Also by the same vessel, from

TWO TO THREE TONS OF NEW POTATOES

Parties requiring cider should order at once as the demand is active.

BRIDPORT ARMS INN, BRIDPORT HARBOUR JULY 18 1855

ADVERT

Good News for the Afflicted Dr Roberts' celebrated ointment called

THE POOR MAN'S FRIEND

Is confidently recommended to the public as an unfailing remedy for wounds of every description, a certain cure for ulcerated sore legs, if of twenty years' standing, cuts, burns, scalds, bruises, scorbutic eruptions, pimples in the face, sore and inflamed eyes, sore heads, cancerous tumours &c and is a specific for those afflicting eruptions that sometimes follow vaccination. Sold in pots at 1s 1 1/2d and 2s 9d each...Observe! No medicine sold under the above name can possibly be genuine unless 'Beach and Barnicott, late Dr Roberts, Bridport' is engraved and printed on the stamp affixed to each packet.

JAN 1861
BRIDPORT TELEGRAPH – We have much pleasure in being able to state that the communication between Bridport and the rest of the world is about to be made even more complete than it was made by the opening of our railway. The electric telegraph is stretching out its arms in this direction, and will speedily embrace us, and recognize us as a member of the great family of cities and states which it has so closely bound together.

MAY 1862
(weekly circulation 4,600)
LYME REGIS, MARINE PARADE – Now that the summer appears to have paid us a fair promise of a lengthened visit, the favourite resort is in such a state as to be a disgrace to any town, much more to a town professing to be a fashionable watering place. Nearly half of the walk is covered with mud and dirt which about two months ago slipped from the cliffs above. We hope that the waywardens do not intend to saddle the parish with the expense of keeping other landowners' property in good order but to enforce (as they ought to have done some time ago) on the owners of the lands adjoining our Marine Parade to drain and keep it in order and not place the chief attraction of our town in imminent danger of being forced into the sea.

DECEMBER 1863
CHARLES Marsh, a boy of 13 years, the son of Mrs Marsh, a widow, daughter of Mr Tucker, of Ford Farm, Netherbury, was summoned for stealing a 2lb bottle of sweets from the shop of Mr Roberts, baker and confectioner, of Bridport. It appears several boys were around the shop window on December 14 and they persuaded the boy to go in and take sweets. Mr Day asked the magistrates to send the boy, without convicting him, to the Industrial School in Bristol, conducted by Miss Carpenter. He believed that, up to now, the boy had been a good boy. He had been brought up expecting to have money to take a farm but when Mr Marsh died and he found the state in which they were left, he went to work at Pymore Mill and took home to his mother every farthing he earned. Mr Day did not make his application professionally, but out of commiseration knowing the family circumstances. The Bench ordered the boy to be sent to the industrial school for five years and expressed the hope that when he returned he would be a good son and a comfort to his mother.

The first year of News

FROM PAGE 11

MARCH 1864
WE congratulate the committee of the Literary and Scientific Institute on the satisfactory result of their negotiations with regard to the transfer of the building.

It is well know that the fine edifice, one of the principle ornaments of the town, was built by Mr Henry Warburton, then member for the borough. It has always been believed that he intended to make a free gift of it to the town, but he did not execute the transfer during his lifetime and made no intimation of his wishes for the guidance of his heir, Mr HW Elphinstone.

The committee, however, succeeded in proving to the satisfaction of that gentleman, what Mr Warburton's original intentions with regard to it were; and he, in the most generous manner, at once signified his desire to carry them into effect.

Much delay ensued on account of the legal difficulties in the way of making the transfer.

These have been now, happily, surmounted, and the building is rested in trustees for the period of one thousand years to be used for the purpose of a Literary and Scientific Institution.

In case of it ceasing to be so used, it reverts to Mr Elphinstone or his heirs.

AUGUST 5 1865
DRUNK AND RIOTOUS – James Hutchings was charged with being drunk and riotous at Burton Bradstock. Prisoner said he had been fishing; on coming back he had gone into the Three Horse Shoes Inn, there a man aggravated and challenged to a fight. PC Cheeseman said prisoner had been turned out by the landlord, but wanted to go back in and fight the man. Fined 5s and 7s costs.

JANUARY 1866
EMIGRATION TO QUEENSLAND
ALL persons paying their own full passages to the colony of Queensland receive a £30 Land Order – equal to 30 acres of land – for each member of their families of 12 years and upwards, and a £15 Land Order for each child between 12 months and 12 years.
FREE AND ASSISTED PASSAGES
Are now given without restriction as to age, to persons of the following occupations – shepherds, ploughmen, road-makers, quarrymen, professed gardeners, miners, carpenters, masons, bricklayers, blacksmiths, wheelwrights, shipwrights &c, also female domestic servants of good character.

for stealing peas from a field in Allington, occupied by Mr John Marsh. Julia Garland did not appear and was therefore ordered to be committed for one month to Dorchester Jail. Diment and Morris were fined five shillings each and costs, and in default were committed to Dorchester for one month.

WANTED
TEN young men to be apprenticed to Messrs John Cox & Son to learn the shipbuilding business.

THE EGGERTON HILL PICNIC
THE picnic advertised in our last issue came off on Thursday. The day was not one of those glorious and sunny ones that the many lovers of this rustic pleasure like to witness, nevertheless, the weather was very favourable.

EXTRAORDINARY CROP OF POTATOES
MR C Hoare of Allington Mills, dug from under one stalk (of the Demarara kidney sort) 118 potatoes, 80 of which were very fine.

TO BE SOLD, CHEAP
A VERY handsome to thoroughbred Bloodhound, young and very docile. For particulars apply to Mr Frost, stationer, East Street.

SEPTEMBER

WOMBWELL'S (no 1) Royal Monster Menagerie will exhibit at the following places – Monday, Tuesday and Wednesday at Crewkerne; Beaminster, Thursday; Bridport, Friday and Saturday next, on their way to Weymouth and Dorchester, Blandford, and Shaftesbury, for Reading Fair, Berkshire.

This stupendous collection of wild beasts, birds and reptiles has not visited this part of the country for the last 20 years.

To expatiate on the merits of this Monster Menagerie is superfluous; it is certain that it contains every variety of the animal world that can be procured abroad, or kept alive in this country. Novelties are profuse.

The gnu, the flying families of squirrels, opossums and phalangers, two mammoth elephants, lions of all ages, sizes and species, tigers, panthers, leopards, pumas, bears and wolves, with a list of others too numerous to name.

ACCIDENT
ON Saturday a little girl living in South Street accidentally caught her clothes on fire and received such injuries that she expired on Friday.

RAX LANE FREE NIGHT SCHOOL
ON Tuesday last, this school was re-opened for a period of seven months. The number of boys present was about 70, from eight to 16 years of age, not one of whom attend a day school. They appear possessed with a desire to learn, and their orderly behaviour (although coming, as many of them do, from the spinning-walk) we regard as an omen that they are desirous of bursting the fetters of ignorance in which they are bound.

OCTOBER

A GOOD OLD AGE – Mary Downton, living in North Allington, attained the very advanced age of 101 years on October 11. She is blind, but her faculties are unimpaired.

NOVEMBER

THE FIFTH OF NOVEMBER
THIS day was observed in Bridport with the usual large assemblage of people in our streets, who seemed to take the utmost delight in kicking about burning tar barrels, firing squibs, &c, regardless of the fears of the timid, the frightening of horses, the risk of setting fire to buildings, or many other disasters which may result from these absurd practices.

PLOUGHING MATCH
THE usual ploughing match which has for several years been contested at Melplash, will not take place this year, but there will be a meeting and dinner at the Melplash Inn, on the 26, when the Rev E D Butts will preside, and arrangements will be made so that next year there will be prizes not only for ploughing but for turnip hoeing, hedging and long servitude.

DECEMBER

INQUESTS
SOME inquests have been held by SS Cory Esq of Bridport, which we are happy to hear have been followed by improvements likely to improve future accidents and preserve life. At Bridport Harbour, Wm G Reader of Yeovil, was drowned whilst bathing some time ago (as stated in our paper). The jury returned a verdict of 'accidental death' and accompanied their verdict with a memorial, requesting the coroner to forward it to the proper authorities and try to procure some means to save life on such occasions. The coroner has exerted himself to such effect that we are pleased to say lifebuoys, ropes, &c, are now always ready at Bridport Harbour to prevent accidents and preserve life in future.

GAS, OIL LAMPS AND CANDLES
ES KNIGHT
begs to introduce to the notice of the public a new

LIGHTING WICK

applicable wherever a light may be required, the peculiar advantage of which, consists in its not being liable to drop, to the irreparable injury of Clothes and Furniture, as is the case with articles manufactured of wax. It is easily lit, burns freely, and will be found ultimately cheaper than most other materials now in general use for the purpose.
*Sold in Balls,
at 9d and 1s 6d each,*

E S KNIGHT, CHEMIST & C, WEST STREET, BRIDPORT

JANUARY
1856
Grammar School, West Street
Conducted by Mr John Beach (of the university of London)
At the above establishment, Young Gentlemen are prepared for the Universities, or for general and professional life. The course embraces the Classics, Mathematics, Natural Science, and the general subjects of a complete English education.

REMARKABLE METEOR
A MOST remarkable phenomenon was witnessed in this town, on Monday afternoon, at ten minutes to five o'clock.

After its disappearance, the space through which it descended was marked by a bright, luminous, pillar of fire, perfectly sharp and clearly defined at the edges, and gradually tapering at each end.

This remained perfect for two or three minutes, when it gradually became less distinct, until by degrees it gradually melted into a cloud of light.

PLEASE TURN TO PAGE 13

E WHITE
Grocer and Tea dealer
SOUTH STREET, BRIDPORT
respectfully informs the gentry and inhabitants of Bridport generally that she manufactures

SAUSAGES

of superior quality by machine, every Wednesday and Saturday in the summer and every day in the winter

WIDE PAVEMENTS: Market Day in South Street before the 1900s (BM)

The first year of the News

FROM PAGE 12

MAY

PROCLAMATION OF PEACE
IN most towns, this auspicious event has been officially announced with due form and ceremony; processions have been formed, in which the mayors, the town clerks, the aldermen and corporations, have appeared in their robes of office, and perambulated the town. But our ancient and loyal borough has allowed the event to pass off without notice – except the proclamation in the usual places – not even were the flags hoisted nor the bells rung! We suppose the town is reserving its powers for a grand display on some holiday yet to be appointed.

A special meeting of the Town Council was held in the Council Chamber, on Tuesday last, at 12 at noon, to hear the report of the Committee appointed at the Quarterly Meeting, to confer with Mr ES Knight and Mr Beach on the subject of illuminating the Town Clock.

CELEBRATION OF PEACE
WE scarcely think the proceedings in this town on Thursday last, will justify our using the headline we have given to this paragraph. What was done on the occasion (with two or three exceptions) would have been quite as appropriate on a fast-day as on a feast-day.

The shops were closed (as on a day of humiliation) but with the exception of flags being hoisted on the Town Hall, and at St Mary's Church and also at the residence of Mr Graves, there was no outward and visible signs of a day of rejoicing. Neither was there a general suspension of business. Messrs Gundry and Co gave those in their employ half-a-day's holiday, but otherwise things went on 'much as usual'.

Burke's
PATENT COMBINED VENTILATING HAT

8s, 10s 6d, 12s 6d

S Stephens begs to call attention the above valuable improvement which has just been introduced in FRENCH HATS by the Inventor and Patentee. The Patent Combined Ventilating Hat will be found quite equal in quality to those manufactured on the old plan, and as the Combined Ventilator admits the air to the forehead, as well as to the top of the head, it will ensure that degree of comfort to the wearer which has so long been wanting in almost all descriptions of French Hats

Sole Agents for Bridport
S STEPHENS, DRAPER, TAILOR AND OUTFITTER, EAST STREET, BRIDPORT

LYME, CELEBRATION OF PEACE
THIS event came off in a style that reflects the highest credit on our town and must make some other towns in this neighbourhood that we could name, of much greater pretensions, 'sing small' on the occasion.

The children of the different Sunday Schools were treated to cake and tea, of which they partook in the street, where the necessary accommodation was prepared. There was boat rowing and a variety of mirth-provoking diversions on the beach, such as jumping in sacks etc etc.

The band also turned out, and by its efficient services contributed to increase the pleasures of the day – the church bells pealed forth their lively notes – cannons were fired, and flags were hoisted at every customary position.

But the great event, was the illumination in the evening, which was a beautiful and remarkable display. Mr Brown's tasteful design, illuminated by gas, attracted attention.

The poisoner William Palmer was found guilty of willful murder and was sentence to hanging.

JUNE

Beach and Barnicott dispensary:
MEDICATED GINGERBREAD NUTS
a safe, pleasant and effectual remedy for Worms.

SEPTEMBER 1867
SYMONDSBURY – The long promised school treat, to commemorate the laying of the foundation stone of the new school, which has been delayed owing to unavoidable circumstances, took place on Thursday last week in the rectory grounds. The bells rang out a merry peal; Mr Stephens's Burton band enlivened the village with their merry strains, troops of children marched two and two through the village, to the scene of the action, where a regular onslaught was made on the cake and tea.

OCTOBER 1868
RE-OPENING of Broadwindsor Church: Through the kindness and liberality of Major Malan, son of the Rev SC Malan, the respected vicar, the parish church at Broadwindsor has been beautifully restored, or rather, we might say almost entirely re-built, for very little of the old edifice, save the tower, now remains.

JUNE 1869
CORONATION DAY, Monday, the anniversary of the coronation of Her Majesty the Queen, will be a general holiday throughout the twn.

The shops are to be shut, and the diversions in Mr Miller's field on the East Road will afford a capital afternoon's amusement should the weather prove to be propitious.

There are to be pigeon shooting matches, horse races, donkey races, athletic sports and a number of amusements and the prizes offered are such as to induce large numbers to compete.

AUGUST 1871
A GENERAL meeting of the the Bridport Association for the Preservation and Improvement, where practicable, of the Ancient Public Footpaths, established July 22, 1870, was held in the Council Chamber, Town Hall, on Monday.

This excellent institution has for its praiseworthy objects, according to the rules, the erection of seats, the embellishment of the public roads, the retention of the whole of the footpaths in the neighbourhood of Bridport, the removal of obstacles such as gates, bars, stiles, and other obstructions places across the footpaths, the preservation of the whole of the beautiful walks in the locality, and the attainment of all these ends, as far as possible by moral means.

JANUARY 1872

TOM Bishop Courtenay, who was charged, a fortnight ago, with neglecting to have his three children vaccinated, has been committed to prison for 14 days, in default of his paying the fine. We hope this will be a warning to the people who, from sheer obstinacy, refuse to comply with the requirements of the Vaccination Act.

MARCH 1873

MISS Beedy MA (Antioch College, Ohio, USA) delivered a lecture on Women's Suffrage, at the Town Hall, Bridport, on Friday evening last. The mayor (T Beach Esq) presided. There was a large and crowded attendance – the ladies especially predominating in the front seats, but on the whole there was about an equal proportion of both the fair and sterner sex.

MAY 1874

WE were visited with a sad catastrophe last Tuesday morning, the result of which was that the large factory premises, near the church, belonging to Lord Rivers, and under the proprietorship of Mr J Andrews, were totally destroyed, together the major part of the valuable machinery and working material they contained.

FEBRUARY 1875

Letter to the editor:
PRICE OF GAS
DEAR SIR – When I read of our Gas Company having at their last meeting declared a dividend of 7 fi per cent, I thought surely there will be a reduction in the charge for the artificial light they supply but I find people complaining that from some inexplicable cause their bills are higher than ever; so that I suppose there is some hope for me yet.
PETROLEUM,
Bridport.

JANUARY 1876

SKATING rinks are becoming very fashionable in many part of the country and it seems likely that Bridport will 'keep pace with the times'.

We hear on very good authority that negotiations are pending for the engagement of the Drill Hall and a splendid rink no doubt should be made there. We believe the matter will be decided in the course of a day or two.

Should the hall be let for this purpose it will be a matter or regret to some that they will lose their best hall in the town for concerts and entertainments.

ECONOMY MEASURE: The stone-built union workhouse was built in 1836 to put the poor to work and save money. It later became an infirmary and then a geriatric hospital   (MH)

The Bastille in Barrack Street

UNTIL 1834 the poor were provided for by a motley collection of private charities, almshouses and parish rates.

The Elizabethan Poor Laws, which treated paupers as criminals, or, at best, idle nuisances, still held force in the early 19th century.

Since each parish was responsible for maintaining its own poor, great efforts were made to drive out paupers who were not a legitimate charge on that parish, and unfortunate individuals were hounded out of the parish bounds.

The laws of 1597 and 1601 enacted that each parish was to provide its sick and aged poor with relief in cash or kind, while the idle poor were to be set to work in Houses of Industry.

During the early 19th century several factors, in particular the effect of rapid industrialisation, led to a massive increase in the numbers of 'able bodied' poor drawing on the parish rates.

In counties like Dorset such individuals would have been primarily farm labourers, many of whom had lost their livelihood through introduction of certain types of machinery, or whose wages were so low that they had to be supplemented. Many of those involved in Dorset's cottage industries – such as spinning, weavers and rope making – were similarly affected.

In 1834, the Poor Law Amendment Act was passed in the interests of greater efficiency and economy.

But what was seen by government and ratepayers as a major administrative reform, became to the workforce a notorious instrument of oppression.

The new law empowered parishes to form unions and set up large workhouses, widely nicknamed 'Bastilles' because of their prison-like appearance and harsh regime.

The aim was to economise by reducing the amount of money given out in poor relief by putting paupers in an institution instead and to reduce the number of paupers applying for relief by making workhouse life unpleasant for the 'able bodied' pauper – based on the assumption that they were idle from choice. The workhouse system was not officially abolished until 1929 and many of the buildings became infirmaries.

Ironically, many of these former workhouses have now been converted into luxury, expensive apartments.

Such is the case with the former Bridport Workhouse in Barrack Street.

The stone-built union workhouse, later known as the Poor Law Institution, was built in 1836. It housed 250 inmates and was managed by a master and matron with the services of a chaplain, medical officer and schoolmistress.

It became an infirmary after 1929 and then a geriatric hospital, Port Bredy, after the National Health Act was passed in 1948.

Source: Dorset Workhouses, Dorset County Council 1980

CLOSE KNIT: A typical scene in King Street, Bridport, during the late 1800s   (BM)

Town Hall and the pavements!

ROOM TO IMPROVE: In 1856, Bridport's Town Hall was seen as in need of major repairs. The town council contemplated extensive repairs, that included removing the roof with thorough renovation inside and out. But when costed it was found to be too expensive (MH)

SEPTEMBER 1856 … Bridport as a town, is, in many respects, open to improvement.

Much has been done of late years in the erection of handsome buildings for schools – the formation of a Railway &x &c – but little in the way of beautifying, or in the simple improvement of its appearance.

There are two objects that afford simple scope for this – the Town Hall and the pavement.

It may not be generally known that about twelve months ago, the Town Council contemplated extensive alterations and improvements in the Town Hall, by the removal of the roof, and a thorough repair of the exterior and interior – but on a preliminary inspection by an architect it was found that these would be attended with much great expense than the borough funds would meet.

The matter, therefore, dropped, and up to the present time, that building which should be the ornament and pride of the town, has been getting worse and worse, and continues an object of astonishment to, and subject of remark by, every visitor.

We are glad, however, that the Town Council has determined if all cannot be done that could be wished – as much as possible shall – and a tender has been accepted for the purpose of putting the interior into decent and respectable condition.

The first thing that arrests the attention of a stranger on entering the borough, is the open appearance of the streets. The second – if he should perambulate the town – is the wretched condition of the footpaths (especially if he should be one of those unfortunates who are troubled with tender feet).

Variety is charming in a landscape, but anything but pleasing in the up-and-down, in-and-out pavement, which our town presents to view.

- *The Town Hall opened in 1786, designed by William Tyler with the cupola and clock added two decades later.*

Thirty seven butchers stalls were accommodated on the ground floor – later replaced by one butcher's shop and the lavatories.

Wide streets are traditionally linked with the existence of markets.

AUGUST 1877
Letter

MR EDITOR – I was pleased to see in your last issue that the Bridport Town Council had appointed a school inspector and were going to put the compulsory clause into effect, a striking contrast to the apathy shown in Lyme on education matters.

We have an Attendance Committee who do nothing, and the clauses of the Education Act of 1876 are dead letters here.

Let us hope that our Town Council will take a lesson from the sister corporation.

The necessity for putting the same into operation in Lyme is see from the fact that on Tuesday two out of four witnesses who were to be bound over to appear at the next Dorchester sessions could not sign their names, and the number of children who are running about the street, fields and shore side the day long –
IGNORAMUS

APRIL 1878

A STAINED glass window has been placed very recently in St Peter's Church, Eype, by the children of the late Mrs Pitfield, in memory of their mother.

Not only is it very gratifying to note such a mark of affection but the window itself is a very great ornament to the church itself.

AUGUST 1879
NETHERBURY FRIENDLY SOCIETY AND SICK CLUB

ON Monday the anniversary of these societies was held, and the members were favoured with fine weather.

The village exhibited a few decorations here and there and flags were hoisted on the church tower and on the house of Mr Hile, the secretary, & c, while festoons of evergreens and flowers graced other portions of the village.

The Beaminster brass band was engaged for the occasion, under the leadership of Mr George Swaffield, arrived in the village about nine o'clock, and made calls at the residence of Mr W Macey, of Clenham, the Treasurer, at the Vicarage, and then to Slape, the residence of FW Gundry Esq, and back to Hatchlands, the residence of Major Griffiths, returning thence to the Cross, and to the Secretary's and thence to the New Inn.

MARCH 1880

BRIDPORT FAIR – A correspondent asks us to use our influence to get the fair held this April in some other part of the town than South Street.

He complains of the incessant noise and asks if the fair was removed from West Street because it was annoying to certain gentlemen, if it is not reasonable that some South Street people may ask to be relieved this year and that the great noise be shared alternately between East Street, West Street and South Street, although he would be glad if it could be removed to some field outside the town.

JUNE 1880

THE annual fair and races on Lambert's Castle Hill took place on Wednesday, when the weather, unfortunately, was anything but propitious.

A dull and cloudy morning was followed by a foggy atmosphere, with drizzling rain, which gradually increased in intensity until the hill was enveloped in a heavy ring of mist.

There were intervals of comparative clearness, but on the whole, the day was a most uncomfortable one. Still there was a considerable number of people on the hill and everybody seemed to endeavour to make the best of it.

JUNE 1880

LENGTHY and heated discussions took place over the rector's, the Rev EJ LB Henslowe, decision to sack the bellringers for going against his orders and ringing out to celebrate the result of the local election. He had called on Canon Broadley at Bradpole when to his 'intense amazement and very great consternation' he heard the bells of Bridport Church ringing.

He went straight home and went to the belfry door, when up the stairs he heard peals of laughter and cries of 'Warton for ever'.

He said he was utterly disgusted at hearing electioneering cries coming from the belfry when he had been doing everything possible to raise the religious tone of the parish.

MARCH 1881

AT last it seems the sun is going to shine on 'friendless' Marshwood. An influential meeting was held there on Tuesday the 15th, when the archdeacon, the rural dean, the Rev E Peek; the Rev FE Allen; the Rev J Going; Canon Woodcock; Messrs Wyatt, Fowler, Hodder, loving and the diocesan architect, T Crickmay Esq, attended and it was resolved to build a new church, costing £1,000.

BEATING THE TRAFFIC: Cycling has always been one way to avoid Bridport's clogged streets   (BM)

Who was the Boneshaker?

BRIDPORT Cycling Club was formed at a meeting in the King of Prussia Hotel on March 11, 1892.

It was a time when cycling was becoming more and more popular.

By 1877, bicycles had come a long way from the boneshaker machines of the past. Light tube frames and ball bearings had been introduced and, as a result, bicycles became lighter, easier and faster to ride.

Before long, bicycles were being ridden at 20 miles an hour.

By 1881, there were over 1,000 firms in Britain making cycles and equipment.

In 1888, JB Dunlop invented the pneumatic tyre, which soon replaced the solid rubber or hollow rubber cushion tyres previously used.

In 1896, cycling was a key part of the first modern Olympic Games.

The first Olympic road race was held over two laps of the marathon course.

Bridport's club was formed at the local headquarters of the national Cyclists' Touring Club, founded in 1877 to provide riders with maps and advice and to encourage the putting up of road signs.

Mayor Mr WAE Hay presided and the Bridport News was soon running regular cycling reports compiled by the mysterious 'Boneshaker', whose humorous writings are a joy to read.

It is thought the first 'Boneshaker' could have been honorary secretary James A Hounsell who put the fixtures in the paper.

There were at least two Boneshakers – one appears to have been killed in a road accident and another sent surreal reports from the Boer War as the world entered the 20th century.

JULY 6 1894
LIGHT YOUR LAMPS

LAST week a lady on tour passed through Bridport wearing the latest rational costume.

Although, perhaps, knickerbockers, jacket and cap do not look very feminine, still they must be more comfortable than the usual long skirts etc.

She was quite an object of curiosity.

Boneshaker

MAY 19 1899

SADDLE UP: Ladies! Ladies! Why do you thus merit reproach? There are 36 of you in the ladies section of the Bridport Cycling Club and yet you could only muster a paltry two for the run to Litton last Thursday. I am ashamed of you, I am indeed. Much, as I regret, to be ashamed of my sisters, my cousins and my aunts. You have your handbooks, have you not? Then why don't you look at them and help to make those very pleasant runs of the ladies' section, pleasanter by your presence?
Boneshaker

Extraordinary charge of bigamy

A NETHERBURY woman with three husbands, Sarah Biles, 36, was brought up in custody of the police on a charge of having feloniously intermarried with William Locker, at All Saints' Church, Southampton, on August 9, 1880, George Biles, her first husband being then alive.

Mr JH Jolliffe, of Crewkerne, appeared to prosecute on behalf of Willim Locker, who instituted proceedings against the prisoner.

The prisoner, who was accommodated with a seat in the dock was undefended. She is a woman well-dressed and of buxom appearance and carriage.

She was apprehended at Blandford, where she is stated to have been filling in a situation as housekeeper … the first marriage was contracted at the parish church of Netherbury, between Sarah Gilham (the maiden name of the prisoner) and George Biles.

They afterwards lived together in Netherbury and had several children but after a few years they separated, the man going to America and the children being put into the Beaminster Union … she cohabitated with another person named James Watts and was afterwards married to him … they came back to the neighbourhood of Beaminster where after a time a separation took place … the prisoner fell in with Mr Locker, the prosecutor, at Southampton sometime afterwards … the magistrates formally committed her for trial at Dorchester.

Rights for women

VICTORIAN women had few civil or political rights.

A wife had to do as she was told by her husband, who was her protector and adviser. Until 1884 a wife was officially listed as one of her husband's possessions.

Victorian women were expected to live up to an image of 'the perfect being' – beautiful, demure, loving and intelligent. Many women actively agreed with this attitude

As the 19th century progressed, women were given a number of civil rights, including the right to vote in local elections. But by 1900 they had still not been given the right to vote in Parliamentary elections.

Women finally won that right in 1918 after the Great War.

Tales of drama on high seas

TRAGEDIES were all 'frightful' and there were frequent tales of drama on the high seas.

Letters were often anonymous but very learned.

The News was regularly annoyed, if not a little outraged, by the antics of people on bonfire night.

The front page of the paper, after the first year, was full of advertisements for cure-alls, the latest in fashion and furniture. Page two contained the railway timetables.

Children were often horribly burned after falling into unattended fires, drunks were rounded up by the town policeman PC Custard or Pc Lavender and temperance and friendly societies flourished, particularly the primrose league.

News was laid out under parish and town headings.

Long may sporting tradition continue

SPORT has always played a big part in the Bridport News's coverage of events in the area.

Bridport Football Club is almost as old as the newspaper, forming in 1887. Its first secretary was Bob Gilchrist.

Among the first officers was Bert Cornick, who was still connected with game some 50 years later as a life vice-president of Dorset County FA. The gentleman's game of cricket was also popular, with other sports like rugby and bowls creeping into the columns.

In 1949, a young reporter called Roger Bailey joined the staff, fresh from the solicitor's office where he had been working as a clerk.

His own sporting prowess and passion made his writing sing. You could almost hear the roar of the crowd and the sound of leather on willow.

When David Cozens became editor in 1974, one of the first things he did was promote Roger to sports editor.

"I joined the paper as a reporter in 1959," David says. "Roger was doing the sport then and it was very much dominated by Bridport Football Club and Beaminster cricket. When I took over, Roger enhanced that and improved the service and it became the best in the area."

Roger's love of local sport was continued by Terry Collin, who built up the sports coverage.

Terry remembered fondly as a youngster passing a football across to an older Roger Bailey as they walked on opposite sides of the road in Beaminster's Clay Lane.

Roger died in October, 1996, and grown sportsmen wept at his packed funeral because a legend had passed on

Terry, a very handy footballer in his day, carried on the tradition of a talented sportsman-turned-writer.

David Cozens still writes sports reports for the News from Lyme Regis. "Sport brings romance to the little man," he says. "The man in the street can become important in his own environment and identify with the stars."

After Terry's death in October 2002, the News had its first female sports editor, Lisa Youd, who was passionate about all sport and was a particularly good footballer.

The sporting baton was passed to Rob Atkins in March 2005, who has quickly become immersed in the world of local sport, playing cricket for the Bridport 1st XI.

A left-handed opening batsman, he scored his highest ever score this season for Bridport (202 not out).

He trained as a journalist at Highbury College and this is his first job.

"Since joining the Bridport News I have been amazed at the depth of sporting talent in such a small area of West Dorset.

"I never imagined I would be writing about international footballers, shooters, sailors, kick-boxers, biathletes among others inside my first six months.

"I've been warmly welcomed by every club in the area and have been especially impressed with the work done by the sports team at the Sir John Colfox School.

"If every school in the country shared their passion for sport and devotion to the young athletes they possess, England and Great Britain would be even more influential on the international stage.

"Sport is important to the majority of people in the area and therefore it is even more vital to produce informative and entertaining pages on a Friday.

"I'd like to think the quality of the pages has not dropped during my first six months in the job from the previous high standards.

"I aim to continue to give a voice to every sports club in Bridport, Beaminster, Lyme Regis and the surrounding area.

"I believe we are blessed with a rare variety of sports and can therefore cater for the whole of the area's sporting public."

MARCH 1881
WE regret to announce, as one of the disastrous results of the recent gales in the north, the total loss of the brig, 'Why Not', of this port, with her crew of seven hands all told.

It appears that the vessel had been away from Bridport for a considerable time trading in Guernsey and other places, and that when she was lost she was on her way from London to Newcastle in ballast … the crew of seven hands were all lost. They were the following: Capt Thomas Denty, who belongs to East Chinnock, Joseph Jerrard, mate, Joseph Jerrard jun, his son, Simeon Hutchings, William Hutchings, Joseph Gear, all five of Burton Bradstock, and William Tizzard, of Bridport.

AUGUST 1882
THE future of Bridport Harbour – the mayor raised the question of the desirableness of the council taking any steps, now that the railway was likely to be taken to the harbour, to let people at a distance and in country places know that there was such a place as Bridport Harbour, and the attractions which were to be found there. He suggested whether it would be desirable to get someone down to get views of the harbour (laughter). Mr Stephens said there was nothing for the people to eat and drink when they got there, nor any lodgings for them.

NOVEMBER 1883
ON Wednesday evening a well-attended public meeting was held at the Town Hall in furtherance of the objects of the St John Ambulance Association for first aid to the injured, and for the purpose of considering the importance and desirableness of establishing a centre of the association in Bridport.

MAY 1884
ON Wednesday evening, Mr Roberts, fishmonger, South Street, had in his shop a fine specimen on the royal fish, the sturgeon, caught off the coast in the vicinity of Swyre.

It measured 5ft 9in long and was 46lb in weight.

FEBRUARY 1885
WE are pleased to be able to note that Messrs H Bartlett & Spencer, are pushing forward the buildings at West Bay with considerable promptitude.

All the foundations are completed and indeed most of the underground cellars, and in one of the houses the first 'joints' were laid on Monday.

The block runs in a parallel line, across the recently void space opposite the Bridport Arms and the fronts will face that house.

My Kind of Town

APRIL 1886
MARRIAGE OF TA COLFOX ESQ JP
(specially reported for the Bridport News)

THE handsome precincts of the Church of the Messiah, Broad Street, Birmingham, has on many occasions been the scene of joyous events for a hymeneal point of view, but probably few were more so in character, than the fashionable affair which came off on Wednesday morning.

This was the marriage of our esteemed townsman, Mr TA Colfox, to Miss Constance Nettlefold, second daughter of the late Mr Edward John Nettlefold, formerly of the Grove, Highgate, Middlesex, and of Mrs Nettlefold, of Hallfield, Edgbaston, Birmingham.

In a large town like Birmingham, and especially in what may be termed a huge vehicular artery such as Broad Street, much passes over almost without public recognition, but which in other and smaller places would arose a feeling of sentiment and interest.

On Wednesday morning, however, it was potent to the most casual observer that something of more than usual importance was about to take place.

MARCH 1887

VICTORIA and Jubilee will be favourite names for children born this year. We have heard of some, locally, already honoured. Jubilee was considered in the year of the other similar celebration and the commonness of George as a Christian name is due to our long acquaintance with monarchs of that name

JANUARY 1888
THE WORKHOUSE CHILDREN AT DOWNE HALL

THE Christmas season may now be considered over and consequently the treats, entertainments and c, considered due to its honour are now events of the past, and for contemplation in the distant future.

During the past season the inmates of the Union have, by the kindness of local ladies and gentlemen, enjoyed some excellent treats and entertainments, and that given recently at Downe Hall to the children and others, by Mr JMP and Mrs Montague, provided a delightful evening's amusement for them.

A substantial tea was partaken of in the kitchen, the table being adorned with some exceedingly pretty flowers and after tea the children gave songs, recitations and c.

END OF THE RAIL: The News staff go along for the ride. Mary Payne, photographer, is pictured right, next to Roger Bailey (P and MP)

All aboard for a VIP seat on the last train leaving town

THE FIRST sod of Bridport Railway was turned at Loders four days before the very first Bridport News hit the streets.

The ceremony was performed on June 19, 1855, by Joseph Gundry, of the Hyde, Walditch, who was chairman of directors of the Bridport Railway Company.

Afterwards he presided at a dinner at the Bull Hotel. It was such a special day in Bridport that the occasion was celebrated as a public holiday.

The railway was completed two years later. It comprised a broad gauge, single line, some nine-and-a quarter miles long.

It went from Bridport to Maiden Newton and a ticket cost about 4d.

The journey took 20 minutes as the Board of Trade set a speed limit of 30mph because of the gradients and curves in the line.

Its first stop was at Powerstock station (then known as Poorstock) and Toller was added in 1862.

Traffic was suspended for three days in 1874 because the gauge was altered from the broad 6ft to the narrow 4ft 8 1/2 inches.

There were many complaints about the huge clouds of smoke that threatened passengers in open wagons so some of the engine fuel was coke.

In 1884 the West Bay extension was formally opened amid great excitement, with a public luncheon held at West Bay.

Thousands of holidaymakers were ferried to the Bay over the years but as bus travel improved, the train was used less often.

● The Bridport News reported with great pride the opening of the Bridport Railway in 1857 after a series of long delays.

Thursday, November 17, was declared a public holiday. Nearly all the shops were closed and the town took on a festive air.

The line was nine-and-a-half miles long from Maiden

THE TRAIN NOW ARRIVING: The Bridport News staff, above and below, take an historic journey (P and PM)

Trains halted 30 years ago

Newton to Bridport station. It passed through some of the most beautiful countryside in West Dorset, although in the days of steam it was difficult to see out the windows.

In March, 1884, the line was extended to Bridport Harbour, which was renamed West Bay by the railway company. The importance of the harbour as a commercial port had dwindled and its future prospects lay in its redevelopment as a seaside resort.

In September, 1930, the West Bay line was closed to passenger traffic, its promise to transform the resort having failed to materialise.

From December 3, 1962, the West Bay extension was closed to goods traffic.

The railway managed to escape the Beeching axe in 1963 after a fight to keep it open.

The train finally made its last journey on Saturday May 3, 1975.

Today, the station at West Bay is a tearoom, the track to the harbour is a cycle way. In Bradpole, a level crossing gate still remains but the track has been absorbed into gardens and countryside.

Towards Powerstock, the line has become farmland and a nature trail now exists where the Wytherstone cutting once stood. Much of the land towards Maiden Newton has reverted to farm use.

Source: The Bridport Railway BL Jackson and MJ Tattershall, The Oakwood Press 1998

APRIL 1889
POWERSTOCK: On Tuesday Messrs W Morey and Sons, of Bridport, held a sale of farming stock, the property of Mr John Wallbridge, declining business, and the event brought together a large and influential attendance of buyers from distant parts. The business was preceded by luncheon, at which Mr Wallbridge hospitably entertained his friends.

MAY 1890
WE are glad to see, by advertisement in another column, that the Beaminster Brass Band intend visiting West Bay on Whit-Monday for the purpose of playing selections of dance and other music at intervals during the day. We hope that on this occasion the Beaminster men, who we know from experience play extremely well, will receive a full share of support and patronage.

1891
IN THE edition of May 1, for the first time, there were portrait photographs of Sir Molyneux Hyde Nepean, accompanying a huge report about the golden wedding celebrations of the Sir Molyneux and Lady Nepean at Loders. The report had a list of presents, fawning speeches from local notaries and lengthy descriptions of the dinner and festivities.
Not for them the customary question: 'what's the secret of your long marriage' to which the answer is unvariably 'give and take'.

MAY 1891
THE VOLUNTEERS: On Tuesday evening the members of 'A' Company 1st VDBR mustered in St Michael's Lane, and, under the command of Lieut Weld, marched to Eype Down, where several manoeuvres were creditably gone through. The men returned by way of Skilling to the field known as 'Humpty Dumpty' where they were dismissed.

APRIL 1892
YESTERDAY morning a disastrous fire occurred in what is known as St James's Road, leading from Netherbury to Slape, by which 13 cottages were destroyed, four of which belonged to Mr R Symes (Whitecross), two to Miss Hallett (Waytown), two to the executors of the late David Lane, three to Mr Charles Watts, and two to Mr Stone (Milton). There were nine tenements occupied and four untenanted, but all the property was thatched, and to this, no doubt, may be attributed the destruction which ensued after the first outbreak.

I SAW THREE SHIPS COMING SAILING IN: West Bay, where shipbuilding was a local trade (BM)

Reporting from 100 years ago

JANUARY 1893

IT is whispered that a possible developed of the no-crinoline agitation among women may be an appeal to the Princess of Wales on the subject.

Those who most dread a possible crinoline period believe that a single word from her Royal Highness would remove their terrors.

In other words, it is taken for granted that if the Princess of Wales were at this moment to pronounce against the crinoline, there would not be the slightest probability of its adoption in England.

JULY 1894

WHAT THEY SAY: That on the 2nd of July, the day on which all trains first ran through to West Bay, a lady travelled by rail intending to get out at the Bridport station as usual.

That the station being improved beyond recognition she didn't know where she was.

That she went on to West Bay, back again to East Street, and in her bewilderment asked the stationmaster to put her right as she could not find the Bridport station, where the trains used to stop and all passengers get out.

MARCH 1895

MORCOMBELAKE Sunday School: On Sunday afternoon, after evensong in St Gabriel's Church, members and friends of the above schools assembled for the purpose of presenting a handsome marble clock to Mr S Moores, for many years their esteemed superintendent.

JANUARY 1895

ON page 6 we report casualties on sea and land during the recent gale and, unfortunately, we now have to chronicle disasters nearer home, for no less than three vessels sailing from Bridport Harbour have been wrecked, and it is feared that the Lilian has gone down with all hands.

MARCH 1896

ON Tuesday the London daily papers did not reach Bridport until the afternoon and this was owing to an accident to the fast London express from Weymouth.

When running between Weymouth and Dorchester, the axle of the engine snapped. Driver Bankes heard the noise and, applying the vacuum, he succeeded in stopping the train before any injury was done. Both the Great Western and South Western lines were blocked for more than an hour.

Recollections from a newsman

WHEN the Bridport News was planning a centenary supplement in 1955, it received a visit from a former member of staff, Mr H Ebdon, who was an articled reporter between 1902 and 1907 when the chief reporter was Mr JW Rowson.

On leaving Bridport, Mr Ebdon spent some time in daily and weekly journalism. After service in Greece and Palestine during World War I he was appointed first county secretary of the National Farmers' Union in Staffordshire.

When the Milk Marketing Board was formed in 1933, he transferred to London to take charge of the organisation of the regional staff. Later he became deputy marketing officer until he retired in 1950.

This is what he wrote for the News in 1955.

ON A RECENT pilgrimage to Bridport – scene of many of my youthful experiences – I halted outside the News office and was intrigued to read the words 'Established in 1855'.

Then I realised that 50 years ago I helped to prepare the Jubilee number of this newspaper.

When one has advanced thus far on life's journey the passage of time is incomprehensible.

Happily, humans have been endowed with amazing gifts, not the least of which is the ability to store, and instantly recall, mental pictures of one's early life – surely the greatest of all the marvels of creation.

So it is that as I write I can clearly visualise many of the personalities with whom I came into contact half a century ago.

From 1902 until 1907 I was an articled junior reporter on the Bridport News and in addition to sharing the outside engagements with my mentor and chief reporter, JW Rowson, I read most of the proofs during that period.

In those days the News was a family affair. The then proprietor, the late William Frost, urbane, courteous and gentlemanly, made a practice of reading through the 'clean' proofs after they had been corrected and delighted to spot spelling errors that had (unhappily) escaped the vigilance of the proof reader.

His red ink markings so impressed themselves on my memory in the early months of my apprenticeship that I soon began to recognise, half-a-dozen lines ahead, such monstrosities as accomodation, acknowledgement and the like.

Wilfred, his elder son, was about my own age and we were close friends during my stay in Bridport. Raymond, the younger son, was very much the pride of his mother, a most charming and gracious lady.

In addition there were the proprietor's brother, George, an amiable bachelor for many years, his two sisters, who ran the stationery business, and daughter Daisy.

Typesetting was by hand and the paper was produced on a flat-bed reciprocating machine which had to be hand fed. There was a separate folding machine, also fed by hand. How different from the modern plant now installed.

I soon learnt that reports of overnight engagements had to be in the office by 7am to feed the ever-hungry compositors, and as I could never do my best work at the tail-end of the day my usual practice was to turn out at 5am with a refreshed body and clearer mind.

When there was no overnight copy to be written up William Crabbe, the overseer of the printing department, and I often cycled to West Bay for an early morning dip and we were back in time for him to be at the office by 7 o'clock. He was then living at Bedford

Place; I had lodgings at Bedford Terrace and towels displayed at our respective bedroom windows just after 6am indicated that conditions were mutually adjudged satisfactory for the trip.

And now for some more general recollections

WE had then just entered the horseless carriage era. Only the year before (1904) had the Motor Car Act dispensed with the need for a man with a red flag to precede mechanically-propelled vehicles.

Bridport had the distinction of housing one of the most outstanding productions of that Edwardian age – a gorgeous white steam car with outstretched wings owned by Mr EP Gundry.

It used to glide almost noiselessly through the streets of Bridport and even in these days would cause one to turn and give a second admiring look.

But the vintage motor I remember best was the single-cylinder chain-driven governless car type of vehicle in which George Bonfield used to drive Col Robert Williams MP to his election meetings.

George was a real pioneer of the early days of motoring. As often as not he was to be found prone underneath the car doing some running adjustment.

His face and hands were begrimed, his hair tousled and his clothing generously plastered with oil and grease, but we had the greatest confidence in his ability as an engineer – he would always get us there and back.

My own job was to report the Colonel's speeches so we had many runs together.

At the conclusion of the meeting it was George's responsibility to take the Colonel back to Bridehead before returning home to Bridport.

It was a lonely journey and George liked me to keep him company.

So when we had 'dates' at the Western extremity of the constituency we often found ourselves chug-chugging to Bridehead towards midnight.

Supper was thoughtfully-laid on by the butler and then, with great coats tightly buttoned and caps back to front, we scampered down the hills from the heights of Askerswell homewards.

Col Williams' Liberal opponent was a Luton straw-hat manufacturer – Mr Johnstone Haye.

Although he was strongly supported by an energetic band of workers, including WS and ER Edwards, ES Reynolds and many non-conformists – political divisions in those days largely followed religious lines – he was not a strong candidate and his Scottish accent made no appeal in the West Dorset countryside.

By the same token the Wessex dialogue was probably quite foreign to his ears!

It was perhaps providential that some of the interruptions at rural meetings were unintelligible other than to the natives.

One of the most picturesque Bridport figures in the early years of the century was Alexander Meyrick Broadley, barrister-at-law, author and journalist.

Son of a former vicar of Bradpole, he lived at The Knapp, where he possessed one of the finest libraries in the county.

On most mornings he would be driven in Bridport with landau and pair by liveried coachman and footman, making his morning calls and invariably dropping in at the News office.

As a young man he had achieved international fame by being selected to defend Ahmed Arabi Pasha after the Egyptian Rebellion of 1882.

His command of the French language was the deciding factor.

Later he was reputed to be a close associate of Ernest Terrah Hooley, the financier.

In a book on the Hooley Affair, there appeared a cartoon depicting Hooley dancing to Broadley's fiddling – an innuendo which so far as I know was never challenged.

At the time I knew him, Broadley had mellowed but was full of literary energy.

One day he inquired at the office whether there was

LIGHTING UP TIME: The late Jack Hutchings shows how the lamps were lit years ago
(P and MP)

anyone who could assist him. Rowson turned the offer on to me and, being a very impecunious cub, I readily undertook the task.

This it happened that whenever I had a free evening, I would cycle over to Bradpole, take voluminous shorthand notes throughout the evening (during which dinner was brought into the library) and bring home a load of work for transcription. It was again an early morning task – I wonder how many of the youngsters of today would be ready to do a similar round?

At the end of the week Broadley would present me with a golden sovereign which I gladly stored away in the sovereign case which all Edwardians carried attached to the end of their watch chains.

A £1 note in these modern times may not seem a very generous reward for hours of overtime, but the sovereign of those days was probably worth four of the paper money we handle so freely today.

Broadley was an indefatigable writer. He compiled most of the GWR travel books of those days.

I am under the impression he coined many of the attractive titles – such as the Cornish Riviera – which are commonplace today.

Many of those publications were dictated to and transcribed by me as was also one of Broadley's books – The Boyhood of a Great King (Edward VII).

Of the Town Council I remember best WB Northover, several times Mayor and always full of restless energy, WG Cornick – what a handsome man! – and Andrew Spiller, one-time Town Crier who later became Mayor of the Borough.

In the legal profession the leading men of that day were CG Nantes (Town Clerk), his partner FBL Mansell, Austen Whetham and JJ Roper – the latter Clerk to the Guardians and RDC. Of the clergy the

PLEASE TURN TO PAGE 23

APRIL 1897
CHIDEOCK: The Queen's long reign. The committee appointed at the parish meeting, held in March, have been most successful in carrying out the scheme for erecting a new parish clock in the old church tower in celebration of the Diamond Jubilee of Her Majesty the Queen. Handsome contributions have been promised to the amount of about £53 and at the last committee meeting it was decided to order a clock from the firm of Messrs John Smith & Sons of Derby, who recently erected the large clock in St Paul's Cathedral.

JUNE 1898
AT THE Town Hall on Wednesday before F Turner Esq, Mary Baker was charge with refusing to perform her allotted task of work as a casual pauper at the Bridport Workhouse on the 21st inst. Defendant pleaded guilty.

JULY 1899
THE Mayor observed that a notice board should be erected at the west cliffs warning people not to sit too near them owing to the danger of falling rocks. Councillor Northover replied there used to be one, but that was used for the boys to shoot at. It was understood another board would be erected.

JUNE 1900
POWERSTOCK parish magazine: This handy book of reference for facts and figures connected with the parish work was published for May this week and contains the list of soldiers fighting in South Africa for whom the readers' prayers are asked. Reference is made to the Communicants Guild, SPG, Juvenile branch of AOF, Diocesan written Examination, GFS, and the Relief of Mafeking. Altogether a good number.

AUGUST 1901
AS briefly reported last week, Arthur Morgan, describing himself as a whistling comedian, was arrested at a common lodging house at Bridport on the 24th of July, in connection with burglary which took place at the house of Mr John Gage, auctioneer, of Axminster, during the night of the 18th inst. He was taken back to Axminster and on Thursday (the 25th) was brought before Mr R Cornish at the Police Court charged with burglariously entering the dwelling house of Mr John Gage and stealing therefrom the Lambert's Castle Race Cup, a towel, tobacco pipe, a cigar and five penny stamps, the whole of the value of about £6.

ALL THE FUN OF THE FAIR: Attractions like these would attract huge crowds in the late 1800s (BM)
BELOW: Looking west along East Street in Bridport with its wide pavements (BM)

AUGUST 1902

ON Friday, Mrs Mary Ann Salisbury (formerly residing in West Bay Road, Bridport), whose name came prominently before the public a few years ago in connection with the Salisbury baby case, was plaintiff in an action for damages of libel against the proprietors of the Sun newspaper.

On Oct 2 last, when the smallpox scare was at its height, the Sun published an account of a case of small-pox in Lamb's Conduit street, where, it was stated, the mother wandered from place to place with a little one in her arms and carrying infection in every step of her way.

It was only after a four days' hunt that she was run to earth at Bow Street. Mrs Salisbury had lived at 65 Lamb's Conduit for the last three or four years where she had carried on the business of a seamstress, and she complained that the account represented her as a common tramp, wandering from lodging house to lodging house. The child, in fact, had chicken pox.

The jury found for the plaintiff, with £50 damages.

NOVEMBER 1903

WHILE always anxious to open our columns for the full and fair discussion of questions coming before the public, we must enforce upon correspondents the necessity of being as brief as possible in their communications.

We have made this request repeatedly but, unfortunately, it has had no effect, as correspondents still write without any regard to space whatever.

We have recently received many letters on both sides which we have been unable to insert owing to their length. If we inserted all, it would frequently mean the issuing of a supplement, which is a very expensive affair.

The inordinate length of these communications is a serious encroachment upon our space and we again ask our friends to bear this in mind – letters of moderate length are generally read with interest, but very lengthy communications are frequently not read at all.

Ed. BN

SEPTEMBER 1904

MELPLASH Agricultural Society Show: We would just give a last word to remind our readers of this fixture at Beaminster on Thursday next. Given fine weather, everything promises a magnificent display and we hope to chronicle a record show, not only in quality and quantity of exhibits but in gate money.

Rector, the Rev (later Canon) HR Farrer was an outstanding figure – he always insisted that if his sermons were printed they should appear verbatim, so that on festival occasions the general news had to be condensed accordingly!

The vicar of Bothenhampton, the Rev Octavius Watson, was another scholarly figure.

He was witty and always full of humour and some of his poetic musings were cleverly conceived.

In the realm of sport there were the two Zealleys – Jack and Arthur – who were a source of strength to county cricket; Harry Dunn, a great football enthusiast, and Norman Good, whose prowess as a yachtsman took some beating.

And there was that grand old merchant, J Thompson Stephens, who traded with the Baltic and introduced me to Russian vodka.

I cannot conclude this reference to Bridport worthies without mentioning Albert and Alex Stone, two talented musicians, the former was organist for many years at Bridport Parish Church and the latter at Beaminster.

There was also one family which could be relied upon to produce a complete orchestra from within its ranks – Stephen and Arthur Champ were great lovers of music and the children followed in their footsteps.

I was interested to read recently that Miss Esther Champ, who was a member of the group when I first knew it, is again living in Bridport.

One further snapshot of 50 years ago: The Crewkerne bus, four-in-hand – at holiday times sometimes six – with Rowland Tucker handling the ribbons. What a master of the reins and what a thrilling picture in the days when the broad street East and West of the Town Hall were uncluttered with queues of parked cars.

Even in those early days West Dorset had its own motorised 'brake' constructed and driven by Mr Hunt, wheelwright, of Southgate, Beaminster. This motorised public conveyance used regularly from Bridport and West Bay.

In a photograph it was shown parked at Weymouth, with a noticeboard advertising 1s return trips to Upwey Wishing Well.

It was geared down to take any hill and in the capable hands of its originator gave trouble-free motoring to many thousands who experienced their first motoring thrills on one of these trips.

Physically, the main features of Bridport have remained unchanged during those 50 years, but there was a placidity in the first decade of the 20th century which has since been ousted for ever by the coming of the horseless carriage.

The feature which has impressed me most on this latest visit is the finely-laid-out car park in West Street on which the local authority is to be congratulated.

And, Mr Editor, having kept a filial eye on the Bridport News from the time I joined the staff, may I also compliment all of you who are today engaged on West Dorset's newspaper on the very fine issues you are turning out?

The News has passed through many vicissitudes but I regard the present era as producing one of the most creditable examples of provincial journalism.

ROYAL PRIVILEGE: Princess Margaret receives a bouquet from Anne Palmer at the Bridport Charter Pageant in 1953. Her grandfather was the mayor, HRC Palmer (BM)

FEBRUARY 1905

THE scholars attending Beaminster boys' school together with their head master, Mr EA Fletcher, and his staff are to be congratulated on being the first winners of the West Dorset Challenge Shield and the Champion Shield of the County for regular attendance. The Beaminster boys' school was the highest in West Dorset, where, judging by the list of figures given, the competition was very keen, with 99 per cent.

APRIL 1906

AFTER THE FAIR: At the Town Hall on Friday before the Mayor (S Champ Esq) and JA Collins Esq, Edward Smith, a sailor, who had been recently discharged from the Albion at West Bay, was charged with being drunk on the highway the previous night. He was found lying on his face in Rope Walks about nine pm by PC Cuff and being utterly incapable he was taken to the police station. A fine of 2s was imposed but as Smith declined to pay he was sent to Dorchester for seven days.

MAY 1907

IT IS no longer the 'Man in Blue' for the members of the Dorset County Constabulary came out for the first time on Monday morning in their new summer clothing.

These are grey uniforms and look not only genteel and smart but consist of a really excellent fabric and will be light and comfortable in wear during the summer months.

MAY 1908

ABOUT six o'clock on Friday morning Mr Forsey, of West Bay, made a fine haul of some 5,000 bass a little way out west of the piers. This is believed to be the largest catch of bass at West Bay. The fish was purchased by Mr TH Norman.

OCTOBER 1909

TO mark the return to Bridport of Mr and Mrs Wilfred M Frost from their honeymoon in Bournemouth, the employees at the Bridport News offices on Saturday afternoon assembled on the East Road and gave the newly wedded pair a very hearty reception, two large bills with the printed words 'Welcome Home' being displayed as the motor-car, driven by Mr George Bonfield, which had conveyed Mr and Mrs Frost from Dorchester passed the employees also raising lusty cheers. The employees of Messrs H Tuckers carriage works also recognised the occasion by the firing of cannon.

JULY 1910
ON Saturday evening, the band of the Dorset Battery RFA, under bandmaster HB Shephard, discoursed pleasing selections of instrumental music in front of the Town Hall.

MAY 1911
ON Monday the local postmen appeared for the first time in new helmets, similar to those in use in the Metropolis. They are light and have peaks 'fore and aft' as a protection against the hot summer sun.

DECEMBER 1912
AS the bells of St Andrew's Church were being rung for services on Sunday evening the clapper of one of them broke off, and in falling to the ground very narrowly missed some members of the congregation and choir boys who were about to enter the building.

JULY 1913
YESTERDAY morning a boy named Stoodley accidentally kicked a pocket handkerchief which was tied up in a knot and lying in the road in front of Messrs HR Hansford & Son's establishment. From the weight of it he noticed there was something inside it, and picked it up. He then discovered a purse and handed it to Mr Ash, employed by Messrs Hansford and the latter, on opening it, found it to be full of gold, with one or two silver coins and a penny. He at once took it to the police station and left it in the possession of Sergt White. About two hours afterwards a woman came to the police station, giving her name as Mrs William Jeffery and said the money belonged to her...The boy was given 2s 6d as a reward for finding the purse.

FEBRUARY 1914
MR WAE Hay presented his Medical Officer's Report to the Rural District Council in which it was stated that a case of scarlet fever had occurred at Bradpole. As there was room for isolation the case was treated at home. On account of epidemics of measles the Bothenhampton Council school had been closed until the 9th March, the Walditch mixed school until 18th March, the Chideock Council school until 20th March.

MARCH 1915
MRS ARR Suttill of 34; West Street, Bridport, writes as follows: Dear Sir – It may interest you and all sympathisers with the West Dorset Women's Suffrage Society to hear that our very effecting and energetic honorary secretary, Miss H Fenwick, of Down House Farm, has responded to our country's call for the services of very individual, man, woman and child, by giving her services as cook in an Urgency Cases Hospital, just behind our firing line, 'somewhere in France'.

PAST PIERS: West Bay in 1958-1959 and below the view from St Mary's Church tower in Bridport in 1923 (BM)

MAJOR ARTERY: Looking east in the 1930s (BM)

FEBRUARY 1916
THERE are few occupations into which women have not entered to fill the vacancies caused by men being called out to the war, and the latest innovation, so far as Bridport is concerned, is 'lady postmen'.

JUNE 1917
CONSIDERABLE excitement was created in West Street by the uncontrollable fierceness of a bull that was being driven from Messrs Morey's market just before six o'clock on Wednesday evening.

NOVEMBER 1918
THE Great World War ended at eleven o'clock on Monday morning, after lasting 1,581 days.
  The news that the great war cloud that has hung over the world for four years and a quarter had lifted and that the dawn of Peace had come was received in Bridport, announced from the News office on Monday morning, with a feeling of devout thankfulness and joy.

JULY 1919
THE fete arranged in aid of St Swithin's Church heating apparatus on Saturday provided a very pleasant time for the large number of people who supported this praiseworthy object. Mr FC Biddlecombe kindly lent one of his fields for the occasion, and flags were flown from the church and many private houses in honour of the event.

MARCH 1920
THE Beaminster ad District Co-operative Society opened their grocery and provision stores in White Hart Street, Beaminster. *Buy what you want at the show which is controlled by the people for the people.*

NOVEMBER 1921
A REPORT by the County Works Committee was presented by Mr JE Mowlem at a meeting of the County Council and this showed that a sub-committee had considered as to the best method of maintaining communication with Lyme Regis by road if and when the present coast road (which the public were now using at their own risk) slips entirely away or otherwise becomes impassable.

OCTOBER 1922
SHORTLY after mid-day on Friday, North Allington was the scene of much animation. Fire had broken out in the Dutch barn, belonging to the Wessex Flax factories Ltd, at the lower extremity of Parsonage Road, and although precaution had been taken in the provision of fire extinguishing appliances, the building was quickly a mass of flames.

FEBRUARY 1923

THE tempestuous weather and the remarkably low tides has caused the Chesil Beach to assume an unusual appearance.

This annual clearing out of the shingle, welcomed by the fishing folk, leaves the beach with a hard, sandy surface, rarely seen at other seasons of the year.

It is the time when Spanish doubloons and other treasure from sunken galleons are usually are picked up.

MAY 1924

INTERESTING developments are taking place in an attempt to provide electricity at Bridport. On the 16th of April, Messrs Preston, Redman and Neville Jones, solicitors of Wareham in Dorset, acting for MR John George Royce, of St Albans Hertfordshire, electrical engineer, served the Town Clerk with a notice of application to the Electricity Commissioners for powers to supply electricity in the boroughs of Bridport and Chard, and the urban districts of Axminster, Crewkerne and Ilminster, and rural districts consisting of Axminster, Beaminster, Bridport and Chard.

JUNE 1925

THE Bridport Parochial Church Council at their meeting on Monday last, sanctioned the contract for the construction of the Bridport Church House and a start has already been made in clearing the site.

NOVEMBER 1926

ON Tuesday last, the members of Burton Bradstock folk dance class were the guests of the school folk dance class at a party held in the school, Mr and mrs RB Howarth being the hosts.

AUGUST 1927

THE Town Council at a special meeting on Friday evening, decided to accept the tender of Mr TB Gulliver of Parkstone, Dorset, amounting to £864 15s 8d in connection with the widening of the East Bridge and roadway.

The decision was quite a unanimous one, and members expressed the opinion that the scheme, when completed, would constitute a much needed improvement to the town.

ABOVE: Party games at the Rectory with youngsters enjoying maypole dancing (BM)

RIGHT: A serene corner of North and West Allington around 1914 (BM)

ABOVE: A crowd gathers in East Street for a speech by General Booth (BM)

BELOW: Boy scouts raise money for the Titanic Relief Fund on the corner of Folly Mill Lane (BM)

MAY 1928

BRIDPORT learnt with melancholy interest and deep regret of Tuesday of the death of Alderman John Cleeves Palmer, which occurred at his residence, South Street, in the early hours on the morning.

In the town, where his activities were so closely centred, the news of his continued illness was received with that foreboding that is associated with an oncoming public loss, so much so, that when the flow it is not too much to say that the townspeople generally felt a deep sense of intimate loss.

FEBRUARY 1929

A WELL-KNOWN farmer in Loders was surprised on going to his cellar to draw some cider on Thursday last to find the cider frozen in the tap of the barrel.
Our correspondent saw the farmer on Friday pouring boiling water over the tap, which after perseverance thawed, the cider running once again.
Not even the oldest village inhabitants can remember cider being frozen in a cellar.

FEBRUARY 1930

SUCH was the friendly spirit prevailing when the Bridport News staff engaged the staff of Messrs Hine at skittles on Friday evening when, at the close, Mr E Hine senr, expressed the wish that a return game be arranged he voice the feelings of every participant.
More pleasant surroundings for the encounter than the King's Arms Hotel, North Allington, would have been hard to find, for there the alley is excellent and the hospitality provided by Mr and Mrs Curtis ever generous.

NOVEMBER 1931

LAST week witnessed the completion of the new gasholder at the Bridport Gas Works, and it is now in full operation, supplying gas to the town.
The latest addition to the company's plant is 72ft in diameter and 60ft high, with a capacity of 150,000 cu ft and forms and important landmark. Its erection coincides with the centenary of the undertaking, gas being first introduced into Bridport in the year 1831.

JULY 1932

TWO wayfarers, who took milk from a churn at the side of the road and were said to have spoilt the rest of the contents were on Friday sentenced to seven days' imprisonment at Dorchester Police Court.

PROCESSION: Crowds gather to watch the Hospital Carnival on July 20, 1912 and below the opening of the new promenade by Admiral Best in 1929 (BM)

JOLLY BOATING WEATHER: Bridport Swimming Club Gala dress to stay afloat and below children line-up to get their picture taken outside Pier Terrace

(BM)

My Kind of Town 31

TICKETS PLEASE: Double-decker buses go about their business in South Street, Bidport, 1959, in a typical scene of the time (BM)

BRIDPORT RURAL DISTRICT COUNCIL IN 1973-1974

Rural decision makers in the seventies

BRIDPORT RURAL DISTRICT COUNCIL 1973-1974

Back Row. (L to R)
J.King(Deputy Eng.& Surveyor),J.C.Angus(Chief PHI),Councillors J.Norman,C.W.B.Lucas,O.A.Aburrow,Maj.E.Golding,E.G.Fry,Col.H. antan,H.M.Latto,W.McLellan,A.B.Mason.
Middle Row.
G.Yates(Eng.&Surveyor),B,Chant(Treasurer),Miss A.G.Mackenzie Deputy Treasurer),Councillors W.H.Woodward,MissI.M.C.Caddy, Andrews(Clerk to the Council),Dr.E.E.Hodgson(MOH),Councillors G.Willy,R.Wood,V.L.A.Seller(Deputy Clerk)
Front Row.
ouncillors D.Burdon,Miss E.M.Bickford,H.Williams,Lt.Col.H.J.G. eld(Vice-Chairman),A.A.J.Palmer(Chairman),Group Captain F.L. ewall,Mrs.M.E.Densham Smith,Col.R.E.A.Foulger,F.H.White.

BRIDPORT MUSEUM

BRPMG
Ref no EA114

AGE OF STEAM: West Bay Railway Station in 1910 (BM)

ROLL OVER: The ancient ceremony of 'beating the bounds', to mark the parish boundary (BM)

BELOW: Bridport News reporter Roger Bailey, right, takes part in the 'beating the bounds' ceremony (BM)

ELECTRIC EXPERIENCE: When the New Electric Palace opened in 1926, on the site of Stembridge's (above), crowds of people had to be turned away on the opening night because it was too full with 500 patrons

Saturday night at the movies

BRIDPORT'S first dalliance with the silver screen began in February 1912 when the Electric Palace opened in Barrack Street in a building that was once the old artillery hall and is now Bernard Gale's Bridport School of Dancing.

According to advertisements, only the best and animated pictures would be shown

The Palace ably served the community for the next 14 years, until it was replaced by the purpose-built New Electric Palace, opened in South Street on June 14, 1926, by Bridport Mayor Mr F Weeks.

The Bridport News reported: "Monday was opening night and the townspeople gave their support solidly to the new enterprise so much so, that although the building can accommodate 500, a great many had to be refused admission, but it could not be helped.

"These good people, however, have since given their patronage and can almost be looked upon as regular patrons now.

"Everyone spoke in praise of the beautiful interior of the building and the wonderful clarity in which the pictures were shown."

The first show was Gloria Swanson in Madame Sans-Gene.

The 1930s were the heydey of the great Hollywood studios and in December 1934, Bridport's new cinema, The Lyric, opened on the site of the original Electric Palace in Barrack Street.

It ran for nearly 30 years until September 1962.

In 1999, the South Street Palace closed suddenly, reportedly because of structural problems.

The saga was a long drawn out affair and the building is now owned by entrepreneur Peter Hitchin, of Symondsbury.

He has big plans for the Electric Palace, including a Parisian-style brasserie, bar, multi-use stage, removable dance floor, arts bookshop and cybercafe. The auditorium will seat 400 people.

The Bridport News, in September 2005, reported: "It is also planned to create film and video editing suites and a photographic and art gallery.

"Grant aid and sponsorship, from local businesses and individuals, has been sought to enable the project to meet its full potential.

"It is hoped the Palace will build links with similar multi-arts venues around the world to share ideas and show what Bridport has to offer."

WAY IN: The entrance to the Palace and the George Biles murals inside (left) and (right) the framed picture of Bob Hope that no-one could straighten no matter how many times they tried

Pictures: Marion Surry

MAY 1933
IN celebration of Empire Day merry peals were rung from the tower of the Parish Church on Wednesday morning and flags flown from the Town Hall and other prominent buildings in the borough.

The day was fittingly observed at the various schools in the town and in some instances a half holiday was granted.

SEPTEMBER 1934
MEMBERS of Bridport Town Council expressed pleasure at the most encouraging report concerning a year's working at the Harbour that has been presented to them since the undertaking was acquired from the Harbour Commissioners at a total cost of £22,000.

Alderman Travers (Chairman of the Harbour Committee) reported the largest shipping since the war, with correspondingly increased tonnage; extraordinary increase in the sale of sand; unqualified success accruing to the council's efforts at beach development and an unparalleled surplus balance.

FEBRUARY 1935
UNDER a Road Traffic regulation which into came into operation last November it is an offence punishable by a heavy fine to ride more than one up on an ordinary pedal cycle.

Magistrates are empowerd to fine up to £5 in the case of a first offence, and to impose a maximum penalty of £10 in the case of any subsequent offence.

The Bridport Borough Bench, however, took no such drastic measure when on Tuesday they had their first case to deal with under this new law.

Supt Beck had explained that the case was brought forward to 'advertise' the regulation and not with a view of obtaining a penalty.

So the offenders, two Bradpole youths, were let off with a caution.

DECEMBER 1936
THE British Union of Fascists have announced that Mr Ralph Gladwyn Jebb will contest the West Dorset division at the next General Election as a Fascist candidate.

FEBRUARY 1937
(whole page and unusually a picture)

MISS Trifine Weld, sister of Chideock's soldier squire, was wedded on Saturday in the beautiful setting of her family's private chapel in the grounds of Chideock Manor – the Roman Catholic Church of Our Lady of Martyrs and St Ignatius – to Mr Gerard Freeman, a Yorkshire solicitor.

Bridport in retrospect

By Arthur Leonard Townsend

IT WAS a damp November evening in 1952 when the train I had boarded at Maiden Newton on my journey from Paddington steamed into Bridport station. A taxi set me down at the Greyhound Hotel.

It was my first glimpse of the town which was to bestow on me a lifelong connection.

Here I was, a 23-year-old Londoner come to join the Bridport News as a reporter. I had been interviewed for the job by the then editor, a Yorkshireman, Mr Heber Bruce.

It was Thursday – press night – so it provided a timely opportunity to meet new colleagues over an ale or two at the Sun Inn (now the Ropemakers) next door to Frost's in West Street.

At that time the printing works was in a building at the rear of Frost's with a Cossor press and a battery of Linotype machines.

Many is the time I held galley proofs for the reader, a function long superceded along with the linotype operators by the computer in today's newspaper production.

Hot metal type has passed into history. Life for a weekly newspaper reporter in those days left precious little time for leisure, covering functions three or four evenings a week on top of the daytime round, including weekends.

Meetings of all sorts, councils, courts, funerals and special church services, formal dinners and on and on had to be covered for £8.10s. (£8.50) a week.

One job I detested was getting the names of mourners as they filed into church at the funeral of some local bigwig.

It was not unusual for some people to be affronted if you didn't know their name without being asked. And then there were the floral tributes to list.

My first evening job for the BN was to cover a talk and film presentation of AI in cattle at Bridport Town Hall. Artificial insemination was then in its early days.

Human interest stories always lend colour to the local news. One stands out for me. A farmer at Piddletrentide wanted television in his home but they had no electricity.

So he wired up a number of heavy duty car batteries in series to produce the 240 watts required, and hey-presto, he had a clear black and white picture of BBC TV – the only channel available at that time

A notable event in 1953 was the Bridport Pageant commemorating the 700th anniversary of the granting of the town's charter in 1253 by King Henry III.

I still have the programme in mint condition, price 1s., as well as my press pass issued by Dorset County Constabulary.

Princess Margaret was the guest of honour and formally opened the pageant which harnessed the talents of hundreds of local people of all ages in a colourful and well-choreographed display. Alderman H.R.C. Palmer of the family brewing company was the Mayor of Bridport and vice-chairman of the pageant committee. Alderman S.J. Gale was the chairman of the committee.

In 1953 an automatic telephone exchange was installed in Bridport. New telephones with dials came on to the scene and four digit numbers replaced the two we had at the BN when calls were connected manually. At first I got around the town and villages on a bicycle – hard work with 1 in 8 hills such as Chideock and Charmouth. The acquisition of a 125cc BSA Bantam motorcycle made travelling tolerable, even in bad weather.

Now half a century on the general character of Bridport town centre is virtually unchanged. But things do change, especially over 50 years.

Thank goodness there are no high-rise office blocks here. They would be out of place.

But the devil, as they saying goes, is in the detail. Many old shops that I remember as part of the living fabric of the town are now boarded up, derelict.

Old family names have vanished from many of today's shops.

However, the traffic is no busier than I recall as the bypass takes much of it away from the town centre.

The housing estates around the town have grown and

MY KIND OF TOWN, TOO: Arthur Leonard Townsend

JULY 1938
FOR the second time this month the wind, reaching gale force, caused the river to overflow at West Bay on Tuesday evening and between 40 and 50 campers at the Municipal Camping Ground had to find other accommodation when their tents, containing their clothing etc, were partly under water.

SEPTEMBER 1939
AS WILL be seen from an advertisement in this issue, the Bridport Manufacturers' Association have decided to give women and girl evacuees work in the net and twine industry while they are living in the district.

FEBRUARY 1940
INFORMATION has been received locally from the County Air Raid Precaution Officer that anti-gas helmets for babies (up to the age of two years) are now available and after the required demonstrations they will be distributed to mothers.
Similar action will be taken in regard to respirators for small children, whose ages range from two years to five years.

MAY 1941
A GRIPPING and timely sea picture 'Mystery Sea Raider' is being shown at The Electric Palace in Bridport during this weekend.
The film deals with an American merchantman seized by the Nazis, disguised by new paint and false funnels, and used as a 'mother ship' for sea raiders.

OCTOBER 1942
A POST office employee, 50, in the Home Guard pleaded not guilty at Bridport Borough Sessions to unlawfully and with reasonable excuse absenting himself from a parade at which he was ordered to attend as a member of the Home Guard.

OCTOBER 1943
THE Red Cross onions which were grown by members of Beaminster Young Farmers' Club are to be collected at Melplash and despatched to Weymouth and from there distributed to the Merchant Navy.

AUGUST 1944
MRS Neal of Symondsbury, has received news that her husband, Bombadier BA Neal, R a, whose unit was engaged in the heavy fighting in Normandy, is back in this country with a shrapnel wound to his thigh.
A letter from him states that he is progressing satisfactorily.

SERVICE AWARD: Bridport News reporter Roger Bailey, left, presents editor Charles 'Foxy' Harris with a retirement gift
(P and MP)

with them the lines of parked cars, an aspect of the streetscape that was non-existent in the fifties. As the railway became history so did Barrack Street as a traffic link with Bridport station.

Now no traffic enters East Street as it did on my arrival in 1952. Bollards bar entry to traffic.

I have a vivid memory of the level crossing in East Road where trains puffed their way out to West Bay which has given way to a roundabout taking traffic along the bypass in a loop south of the town.

For some months I represented the Bridport News' East Devon edition living in Axminster and covering the town and Lyme Regis as well as the villages in that area.

There was a friendly rivalry between myself and the opposition Pullman's Weekly News reporter Wally Fellender.

At an Axminster urban district council meeting his paper was soundly rebuked over a story. Wally angrily rose to respond: "I am here to report your meeting for my paper, not to accept criticism on its behalf." Good old Wally!

Mind you he would be somewhat put out if I scooped him on a big story.

In the Woodmead Hall at Lyme Regis I joined a large audience of oldies eagerly watching the Queen's coronation on a large screen capturing the historic images on a Decca black and white projection TV.

In winter, despite two pairs of gloves, a long lined leather coat, wellies and a crash helmet I would be frozen by the time I had ridden the 12 miles to Bridport on the Bantam on my weekly trip with the copy for my edition.

Council meetings generally followed a pattern, some humdrum, others lively.

Lyme Regis fell into the lively category and you knew what to expect – a day-long session with heated personality clashes flowing thick and fast with the Mayor, Councillor Mrs BM Staples doing her best to keep order.

Seaton Town Council, on the other hand, was a complete contrast.

Discussion was minimal and it was all over in 15 minutes. Any debate was obviously confined to committee meetings so the monthly council meeting was virtually rubber stamp time. One of the magistrates' court cases at Axminster called for evidence to be given by the police constable from Charmouth.

It highlighted the quite noticeable difference between the Dorset and Devon accent, even over that short distance.

During my first few days when I stayed at the Greyhound Hotel I heard some familiar voices across the dining room from another table at breakfast.

They were of the well-known Dorset farmer Ralph Wightman and Freddie Grisewood, the celebrated wartime presenter of food tips on BBC radio who was now presenting the weekly 'Any Questions' which the previous evening had come from Bridport.

Every time I return to Bridport I see fresh changes. Among them is the county library. I covered its official opening in East Street.

Now it has been moved to new purpose-built premises in South Street which I visited in 2002.

Back in the fifties the Drill Hall was a favourite venue for me and my friends at Saturday night dances.

This was pre-rock and roll, and ballroom dancing – the quickstep, foxtrot and waltz – still held sway. Alas the drill hall is no more.

It was been swept away along with the house in St Michael's Lane where I had digs and the handy little pub – I forget its name – a few doors away.

And the BN's printing works behind Frost's, for years a hive of activity, was a forlorn empty site the last time I wandered round the back.

Now the BN is housed in a modest suite of offices in East Street and printed in Weymouth. In my day it was a broadsheet paper, later to become a tabloid and eventually the addition of colour photos.

With the passage of time few of those I knew in my BN days are still with us today.

My erstwhile colleague and friend was Roger Bailey. Each time I visited Bridport he would bring me up to date with happenings on the local scene, including the occasional scandal.

We would repair to the bar at the Bull Hotel and a few

AUGUST 1945
WHATEVER thoughts and reactions Bridport people may have had concerning the end of the war, first and foremost was that of thanksgiving.

Led by the Mayor and Mayoress (Councillor and Mrs SJ Gale), members of the Corporation, and supported by ministers of various religious denominations, the public's first act in a day of rejoicing on Wednesday was to attend divine service.

SEPTEMBER 1946
LAST held in August 1939 – at a time when Germany invaded Poland and war clouds gathering in Europe the annual show in connection with the Melplash Agricultural Society took place on the Crown Ground, Bridport, on Thursday last week.

The decision to revive the show met with a large measure of support and although the classes were restricted, the number of entries was good.

JULY 1947
BETWEEN Saturday night and Sunday morning a Bridport doctor's case, containing dangerous drugs, was stolen and despite a BBC broadcast appeal, no trace of the missing article has been found.

OCTOBER 1948
CLOSING his shop for the first time on Saturday afternoon, Mr AD Whitworth, one of Bridport's principal grocers and provision merchants, gave a News reporter some of the reasons why he made the decision.

"I found cash purchases to be negligible from a trader's point of view. In the main they were for commodities other than rationed goods," he said.

APRIL 1949
AN Easter invasion without parallel since the war brought holidaymakers in their thousands to West Dorset resorts in constant sunshine during the daylight hours from Friday to Monday. Temperatures topped 80 degrees.

MAY 1950
BRIDPORT'S seaborne traffic is getting back to its pre-war standard and this is despite the fact that the import of gas coal, wood and cement has virtually ceased, for the time being at any rate.

During last year, twenty-four ships used Bridport's harbour, which was only seven less than in 1938, the last complete year prior to the war.

'I'll never regret my special bond with West Dorset'

DOUBLE ACT: Roger and 'Foxy' (P and MP)

other hostelries besides. Apart from the charm of many of the pubs in town and village they were the centres of local gossip and sourced many a story.

A regular in the bar in the Bull in the fifties was Morny Turner. He was never called Mornington. It was always Morny.

He represented the Dorset Daily Echo and with Roger we would yarn about this and that over a pint or two of Palmer's bitter. Morny would have been about 60 at the time, a veteran of the First World War, with a glass eye as a result of his wounds.

Always good company, he would invariably turn up in an old raincoat and trilby hat.

Roger seemed to be a fixture at the BN and knew everyone who was anyone. One time we were walking along East Street when Roger greeted the approaching figure: 'Morning Reg'.

It was the head of the Dorset Knob family baking business at Morcombelake.

"Mr Moores to you Roger," came the stern retort. Typically Roger laughed it off. He always displayed a good humour and I think that sustained him. I last saw him in 1989. Sadly, I learned on my 1997 visit that he had died the previous October.

Every Thursday night involved delivering papers to surrounding villages in one of the two ancient Ford 8s. One of them, of 1936 vintage and long past its heyday, rattled alarmingly as it nosed its way along almost empty roads with its bundles of the latest BN hot off the press.

One of the cars had been painted green with what looked like house paint.

The driver was invariably a young compositor and one or two of us reporters would accompany him, stopping at a newsagent or a village pub to drop off one of the bundles and enjoy a quick beer and sometimes glean the makings of a story.

Soon after I began working at the BN I spent a weekend with friends in Portsmouth.

It coincided with the great smog in London of which I was unaware on my Sunday night return to Bridport. I waited for the train from Waterloo to take me to Dorchester.

And I waited and waited. Eventually it arrived and I got to Dorchester long after the Bridport bus had left.

I couldn't afford a cab so I started walking along the A35 hoping for a lift that never came. Eventually I got to my digs in the middle of the night having completed the 16-miles on foot.

I turned up at the office on Tuesday morning with the editor demanding an explanation!

W hy do I return to Bridport time and again when I worked at the BN for barely 16 months? Especially from Adelaide in South Australia where I have lived for almost 40 years.

I had been in Bridport only a few weeks when I was persuaded by Mr Chapman Andrews, a Bridport Grammar School teacher, to join the Bridport Amateur Operatic and Dramatic Society.

I attended readings but never performed on stage though the young lady to whom I was introduced by Mr Chapman Andrews had been in a number of productions in a variety of roles.

She was a former grammar school pupil who had just returned from a stint as a secretary in London – Doris Hiscock.

A friendship developed, the following year we became engaged and in March, 1954, we were married at St Swithun's Church, North Allington.

We began married life in Ramsgate, moved to Coventry, London, Rhodesia (now Zimbabwe), back to London in the press gallery of the House of Commons and finally, in 1966, to Australia, continuing my career as a reporter.

After my wife succumbed to cancer in November, 1996, my two daughters and I brought her ashes home to Bridport.

These were interred in a plot in front of St Swithun's at a special service in May, 1997.

When I visited Bridport again the following year I was pleased to discover that one of the old buildings to have survived is the house in Crewkerne Court, opposite the Odd Fellows Hall, where Doris and her older sister, Olive, were born.

I hope I can again return to Bridport before I finally join Doris in that plot at St Swithun's where our life together began.

Welcoming, helpful and willing to please, sums up the impression the people of Bridport have made upon me.

When I discovered the attractions of west country life as an 11-year-old wartime evacuee in Somerset, little could I realise that fate would subsequently draw me back to the west, albeit to the neighbouring county. I've never regretted that lifetime bond.

JULY 1951
THREE men from a camp at Maiden Newton came to Bridport to spend Saturday evening. One fought in West Street and was arrested by police. His two friends went to Bridport Police Station and demanded his release. They, too, were arrested. The fight and its sequel were described to Bridport Magistrates on Monday when the three men pleaded guilty to the charges preferred against them.

JULY 1952
TELEVISION arrived in West Dorset in no uncertain manner on Tuesday morning. Shortly after 11 o'clock the new TV station at Wenvoe sent out its first test signals on the waveband which is to be used permanently and the reception in the Bridport area was perfect; indeed it far exceeded the expectations of the most optimistic.

OCTOBER 1953
BRIDPORT Rural District lacks a water supply sufficient in quantity and satisfactory in quality, says the Medical Officer of Health, Dr Adam Armit, in his report for 1952.
Of 32 bacteriological analyses carried out during the year of water from local authority supplies, 20 were satisfactory, four suspicious and eight unsatisfactory.

MAY 1954
BRIDPORT Town Council are to review unilateral waiting regulations. This was agreed at Tuesday's meeting when the Highways Committee reported considerable dissatisfaction with the present measures and the Mayor, Ald HRC Palmer, said it was general knowledge that Bridport's trade had deteriorate tremendously since the adoption of unilateral waiting.

APRIL 1955
THERE were queues in East Street when one of Billy Graham's services at Kelvin Hall, Glasgow, was relayed to Bridport Congregational Church last Wednesday.

JULY 1956
BACK in the good old days one of the biggest sporting evenings in the West Country was the Lambert's Castle Races. People flocked to this famous beauty spot on the Dorset-Devon border to see horses from as far afield as Cornwall and Hereford running. But those days have long passed. And this year, probably for the first time since the meeting began some 150 years ago (with the exception of the two world wars), there will be no Lambert's Castle races. Mr B Gould, hon secretary, said interest had waned with the advent of TV.

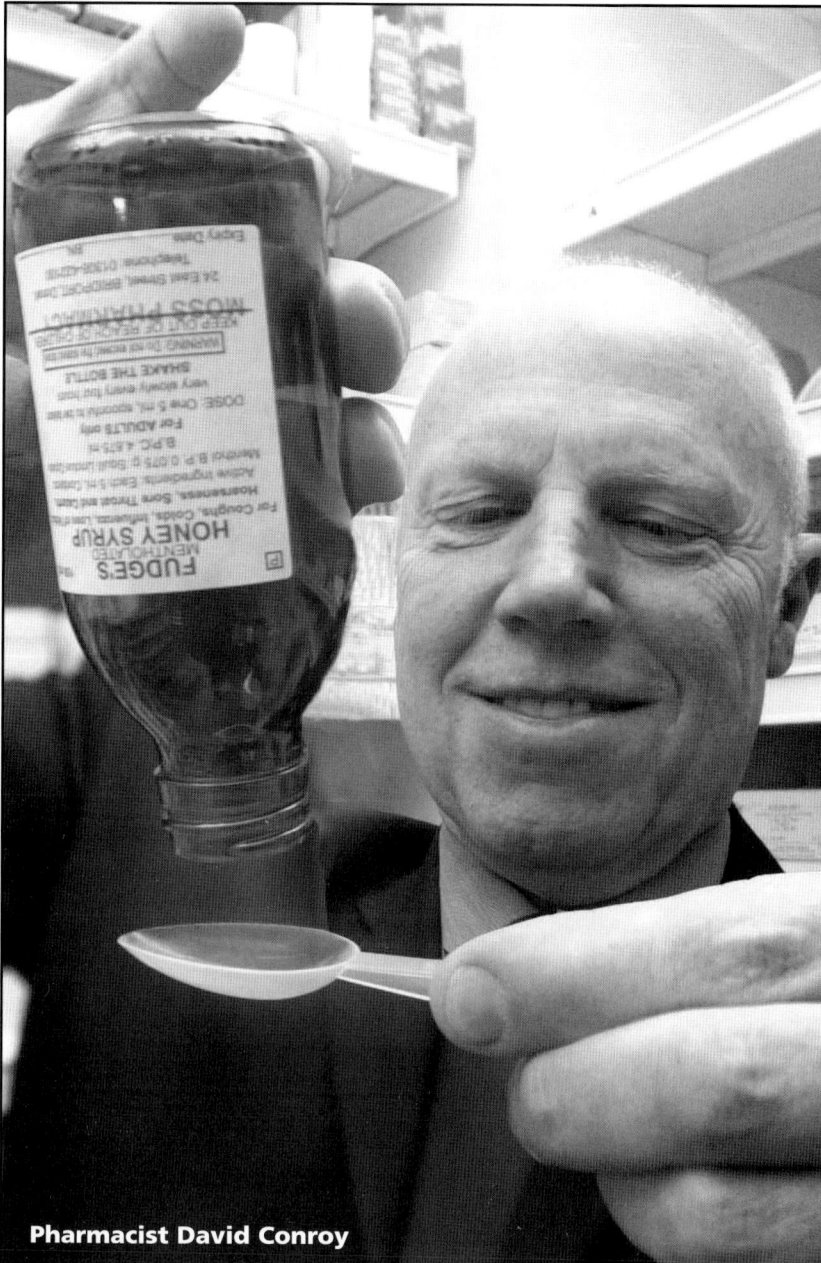

EXPERT HANDS: Pharmacist David Conroy with the historic Fudges cough mixture that has helped generations of people overcome winter ills (BN)

Firewater to cure all ills

ONE of Bridport's quirkiest claims to fame in modern times is that it is one of the few towns in the world to have its own cough medicine.

It is a special one, at that.

Locals call it Fudge's Firewater and it can be bought only from one shop – Moss Pharmacy in East Street.

However, towards the end of 2005, its future was in doubt following the merger of Moss with the pharmacutical giants Boots empire.

Fudges is renowned for curing coughs and hoarseness.

But the medicine is not for the faint hearted. Once it hits the back of your throat you feel like your mouth is on fire – but it helps you forget about your sore throat. Take too much of it and you end up hallucinating.

It is thought to be as old as time but it was invented by Mr Fudge, who was a chemist at West Allington in the 1950s and 60s.

The preparation is made to a secret recipe and customers have to sign for it. Bottles are limited to one per household because it contains opiate.

At times of colds and cough outbreaks, the chemist works round the clock to produce the stuff.

When the poor man can't keep up with the demand, word soon gets around that there is an official Fudge's shortage. Some people stock up in advance of the winter months, just in case.

NOVEMBER 1957
DR A Lisney (County MOH) has sought the help of youth leaders throughout the county concerning the problem of smoking and lung cancer.
"Smoking in the young presents a problem of such important that it cannot be ignored," he told them. Pointing out the 'alarming increase' in lung cancer over recent years, Dr Lisney has appealed to youth workers to help in preventing young people from starting the habit.

JUNE 1958
THE important part which games and athletics in general plays in a boy's and girl's physical and mental development was stressed at a meeting of the Parents' Association at the Colfox School, Bradpole, on Monday evening by Mr JM Pedlar, who is in charge of physical education at the school.

FEBRUARY 1959
THE idea of cutting out the amber phase of the traffic lights at the Town Hall, Bridport, was brought up at a meeting of the Bridport, Lyme Regis and District Road Safety Committee last Friday. The secretary, Mr OD Roberts, told members that experiments are to be carried out by the Ministry of Transport, the Road Research Laboratory and the local highway authorities at Leicester, Wolverhampton, Brighton and Hove and Northampton.
 Mr Roberts said: "We feel that it would be a big improvement if something could be done with our traffic lights at the Town Hall."

JULY 1960
A LONG debate about the behaviour of young motor-cyclists on the roads of West Dorset was sparked off at Friday's meeting of Bridport, Lyme Regis and District Road Saftey Committee when the Chairman (the Rev Lionel Brown) commenting on the June accident report, declared: "It is deplorable that there is such carelessness in so many of these accident cases."

AUGUST 1961
FILMS dealing with nudist camps are not new but it is still a little startling to find 'stills' of nudes outside cinemas.
And perhaps it is a sign of the healthier attitude to the human body that photographs of nudes outside a Bridport cinema during the early part of this week have attracted so little comment. Time was where there would have been indignant sermons from local pulpits and angry questions at the Town Council meeting.
People living opposite the cinema tell us that a few elderly men have 'had their noses glued to the pictures' but although we pass the cinema two or three times a day, we have not noticed any adults or even teenagers who seemed particularly interested.

An editor whose devotion to duty received Royal acclaim

By David Cozens MBE

Bridport News editor 1974-1991

HOSTILITIES in the Crimean War were in their final year when the Bridport News first appeared on the streets of the town.

It did so with high hopes and good intentions and, despite some difficult times, has fulfilled its raison d'etre in every respect.

The voice of West Dorset, the clear market leader in its area, has grown with the march of time and has taken on board the best of the new without compromising its standards of integrity.

Having been connected with the News for over 45 years, 17 of them as editor, I have been privileged to work with many dedicated journalists who have gone on to make their mark in the newspaper world and particularly enjoyed the cut and thrust of competition, particularly in the early days of my career.

When I began, the late Charles Harris – nicknamed The Fox – was the editor, the enigmatic Roger Bailey was sports reporter cum Beaminster reporter, and the late Colin Hoath, who went on to a brilliant career with the Canadian Broadcasting Corporation, was the chief reporter. Big Roger was, of course, a legend in his own lifetime, while Mr Harris was a character and a half.

A former News of the World sub, his boast was that, if a couple kissed at the beginning of the story, he'd have them in bed before the end.

He once amazed us all by leading with a non-story – 'Diana Dors is not buying a house in Bridport' – and he was the source of great amusement when he used to ride through Bridport on a moped wearing a helmet inscribed 'Editor'.

Lyme Regis was my patch, and my first serious job was a meeting of the town council.

Even that did not put me off for I was well and truly smitten with the romance of the profession.

The 'editorial department' – an upstairs room surrounded by musty broadsheet files – was Dickensian.

But it was magic to me and I was quite sad when The Fox was careless with his pipe and burnt the office down!

It was in that room that I rubbed shoulders with one or two incredible individuals, who lasted only a few short months between them.

There was an elongated individual who showed up with a parrot on his shoulder, a one-handed Irishman who took three weeks to write a story and a garrulous visiting sub-editor who quoted a lot of Oscar Wilde and wouldn't let me leave the office until I had spotted and inserted a missing comma in my copy.

JUNE 1962
BRIDPORT Rural District Council are concerned about the proposal contained in the White Paper relating to the new Hospital Plan for England and Wales to close Port Bredy Hospital by 1975.

MAY 1963
MOVES by Labour councillors to get the Press admitted to the council's committee meetings were defeated at the meeting of Bridport Town Council on Tuesday. The General Purposes Committee had reported that a letter had been received from the Bridport and District Ratepayers and Residents' Association notifying the passing of a resolution requesting the council to consider admission of reporters to such meetings. It was recommended that no action should be taken.

OCTOBER 1964
A BOMB has been found on land belonging to Mr Aza Pinney, the 28-year-old West Dorset Liberal candidate.

The discovery was made on Tuesday when workmen were ploughing barley stubble on the slopes of the 909ft Pilsdon Pen, Dorset's highest hill.

Mr Pinney, who farms 400 acres of cereals and fatstock, informed the police and a bomb disposal unit was advised.

Mr Pinney is not blaming his opponents for putting the bomb on his land.

"I think it is probably a wartime relic," he said on Wednesday.

JANUARY 1965
If Charmouth Parish Council has its way, there will be no bingo hall opened in the village. At a special meeting on Tuesday night, the council agreed, by seven votes to three, to write to Bridport RDC requesting that an application for outline planning consent by Mr Reginald Cathcart, who wants to turn his gift-shop into a bingo hall, should be refused.

AUGUST 1966
The Mayor of Bridport (Cllr AB Mason) and the Town Clerk (Mr Marcus Knorpel) flew over the town in helicopter on Friday. They circled the borough slowly and had a wonderful bird's eye view of it. The Mayor told a Bridport News reporter the following day: "We could see exactly what a waste of land there is in Bridport. From the air, it just shouts at you.

"There is a tremendous amount of land in the borough, all crying out for development and none of it bringing it in any rateable value to keep the town's rates down."

LIFETIME HONOUR: David Cozens receives an MBE from the Queen in the New Year's Honours List 2000. He was awarded the honour for services to the community in Lyme Regis, particularly for his work with the National Association of Boys' Clubs (DC)

DECEMBER 1967
FOR thousands of West Dorset folk Christmas may not be quite the same this year. Because of the foot and mouth epidemic that has swept through much of England, the Cattistock Hunt will almost certainly not be coming to Bridport for the traditional Boxing Day meet.

APRIL 1968
SHOULD the Rope Walks Clearance Area be left to look like a derelict bombed site or should it be developed? That was the big question confronting members of Bridport Town Council at Tuesday's meeting. At the March meeting of the Council it was agreed to demolish a large area of Rope Walks and to put in a planning application for the re-development of the entire site for residential purposes.

JANUARY 1969
BRIDPORT has lost one of its best-known dogs. Peter, the nine-year-old boxer belonging to Alderman Percy Norfolk, of the Rax Dairy, East Street, died in his master's arms on Sunday night while waiting to undergo a operation at the local vet's. Alderman Norfolk, with tears running down his face, told a Bridport News reporter: "I am brokenhearted. He was a wonderful old dog and he lived for me."

JULY 1970
A COMPREHENSIVE community centre for Bridport? The idea may come to fruition if an inquiry into the possibility of converting the Methodist Church and its various rooms provides the right answers. The object would be to adapt the premises as a permanent home for organisations of the town – such as the Bridport Amateur Operatic and Dramatic Society, the Pantomime Players, and the Arts Club, to name but a few.

MAY 1971
TEENAGE girls, some around twelve and thirteen years old, are in moral danger on the Fishweir Estate because of the lack of recreational facilities, say housewives. A meeting of the Residents' Association is being called to campaign for a petition to be sent to the council demanding action. The secretary of the Fishweir Residents' Association, Mrs Kay Ashton, 23, said: "I will personally call on every housewife in this area if necessary after what I saw happening last Easter. Now Whitsun is almost upon us. I am no prude and am broadminded but to see those kids of girls – some were nearer 12 than 14 – flaunting themselves in the scantiest of mini skirts and no tights, but briefest of briefs, disgusted me."

After a couple of years, I was sent to oversee Lyme where we had opened an office because of the burgeoning success of the first edition. It was here that I first clapped eyes on Chris Carson, now the chief reporter at Bridport and one the best news journalists in the area. Chris, an eager junior, arrived on his own scooter.

That was impressive because it was better than the transport so generously given to me by former proprietors, Bennett Brothers.

A clapped out BSA motorcycle was plenty good enough for me, said boss man, Daddy Bennett.

They were tough times.

We often worked seven days a week and, indeed, there were occasions when snow blocked the roads that I would walk to Axminster to put copy on the train in the days when we were printed in Salisbury.

Later, when the News was taken over by the Somerset County Gazette group and we printed in Taunton on Thursdays, it was common practice to attend lengthy meetings of Lyme Town Council on a Wednesday, write it and drive to the nightshift in the Somerset town, arriving at about 2am.

By that time I was driving a decent car, having progressed from the old Ford Anglia bought with a £75 loan from the company.

It was just as well, took, because my wife used to ride with me in the early hours to make sure I didn't nod off at the wheel.

I became editor at Bridport in 1974 and thoroughly enjoyed my 17 years with the talented staff, including dear old Roger, the memory man – the only punter I know with the gall to ring up a bookie half way through a race broadcast and ask for his money to be taken off a horse which clearly wasn't going to win.

Roger once worked for nothing in the 1950s when the paper hit hard times, and we shall never see the likes of him again.

I still miss, too, my great friend Terry Collin, Roger's successor, whose sudden death is still felt throughout West Dorset.

Working for the Bridport News, which has recorded local stories of national and international importance, led campaigns and reported faithfully on the essential bread and butter issues, has been a sharing experience – sharing in people's aspirations, joys and sorrows and feeling a part of a great little community.

For that wonderful journey, I thank the loyal readers of The News.

Couple made a career out of hobby

Peter and Mary Payne

Freelance photographers 1967-1991

By Mary Payne

IN 1962 we established a landscape and contract gardening business in Bridport.

Our hobby was photography and Peter gained experience with a camera at evening classes and helping Leslie Frisby, who had a business in East Street, with weddings.

In the mid 1960s, Richard Egalton retired to Bridport from London and became the local press photographer after John Clist.

He asked Peter to help out with some of his evening work and as photography was an expensive hobby we were glad to earn some money which enabled us to purchase better cameras and set up a darkroom in our attic.

After a spell in hospital Richard once again retired and we became more involved in press photography.

It was not easy to run both the gardening and photography business at the same time so when we had difficulty replacing two of our workforce we decided to concentrate on photography.

We always worked as freelances, which meant we were only paid if a photo was published or ordered. Payment was also according to the size that the photograph was reproduced in the paper, and was less for a weekly paper than a daily, but it cost us just the same to take the pictures.

The 1970s were one of our busiest times as there were fewer staff photographers and as well as the Bridport News we were supplying the Dorset Evening Echo, Western Daily Press, Western Gazette and Pulmans Weekly, as well as still photographs for Westward and TSW if they were filming in the area.

There were problems in working for so many papers, in those days there was strong competition between the BN and the Echo. Often they each through they had an exclusive story, and when it appeared in both papers we were sometimes wrongly blamed for leaking it.

Also no matter how hard we tried to distribute the photographs evenly the editors often said that their rival had the better photograph.

Experienced journalists such as Bill Harris, Roger Bailey and Ray Barwick, from the Dorset Evening Echo, taught us a tremendous amount about reporting.

They could often find a story to fill a gap in the paper just by walking down the street or a quick visit to a local hostelry.

Harry Mitchell was another from the old school of reporters who could get a tale from the most reluctant of interviewees.

It was interesting to meet young reporters such as Paul James and Steve Hunt in their early days in journalism and watch them develop before they moved on to further their careers.

Other reporters like Graham Taylor and David France moved from cities to Bridport to find that they were not totally suited to a rural life.

Whilst it may be more time efficient for today's reporters to spend more time in the office relying on the telephone and people bringing in news I feel that often stories can be missed by not being out and about and not attending some events.

Back in 1959 I can remember a BN reporter cycling to Waytown and spending an hour interviewing us so that he could write our wedding report.

West Bay has always been a source of dramatic pictures, whether it is flooding, storm damage to the piers and esplanade, or the evacuation of the camp site.

Our most reproduced photograph must be of the 1974 floods taken from the East Cliff with reporters Roger Bailey and Chris Coneybeer standing in the foreground viewing the scene.

I still receive requests for it to be reproduced, the latest being for use on an educational website.

On that morning in February, 1974, we were asked to go to West Bay and take some pictures of the flooding.

We were not expecting anything very unusual and, as Peter had arranged to accompany Jim Spicer

---

FEBRUARY 1972
A BRIDPORT headmaster has banned pupils from riding their cycles to school until they pass a proficiency certificate, because, he says: "Children are being allowed on the roads on fairy cycles even before they can read."

MARCH 1973
SHAPELY Shirley Stone, a 24-year-old housewife from North Allington, will be taking to the catwalk tonight (Friday) on Westward TV. Mrs Stone (measurements 36,26,36) is out to win the 'Miss Westward' beauty crown. She enjoys dancing, driving and crochet.

MAY 1974
A GEORGIAN mansion, close to Bridport's busiest shopping area, must go.

It will be replaced by a car park for 80 vehicles. A compulsory purchase order dating from 1971 on Wyke's Court, North Street, has been confirmed by the Environment Department.

Now the once elegant home has to disappear to make room for a revised traffic system involving Chardsmead Road, Rax Lane, North Street and Downes Street.

MAY 1975
A FAILURE for democracy – that's how the Bridport Railway Action Group summed up the closure of the branch line to Maiden Newton as the last train slipped out of Bridport Station at 8.40am on Saturday evening. Hundreds of railway enthusiasts from all over the country took advantage of the extra carriages British Rail had laid on for the final day in the line's 118-year history.

JANUARY 1976
Bridport's traders are disappointed.

Although their strong representations have succeeded in securing some easement in the crippling parking restrictions imposed about a year ago, they have not achieved as much as hoped for.

Shoppers are still unable to park in vital stretches of the town.

MARCH 1977
BRIDPORT Police will in future oppose all applications for occasional licences which permit the sale of late-night alcohol at discotheques in the town.

Following allegations of vandalism and under-age drinking at local discos, the police will stipulate that weekend disco bar licences must end at 11pm in the winter and 30 minutes later in the holiday season.

My Kind of Town 43

OFFICE FUN: News staff at the East Street offices. Peter Payne is pictured right. His wife Mary is peeping out from the back. The couple took thousands of photos but there are very few showing themselves

on his election campaign, I set off for West Bay.

As I walked down Station Road in water up to my knees with a brand new Hasselblad camera in my hand reality suddenly set in.

On another occasion I was escorted down Forty Foot Way by two policemen, one to stop me from being blown over and one to watch out for flying debris as gales tore off the roofs in the Old Shipyard.

Being involved with the press meant that we attended many events and met many people we would otherwise never had the opportunity to do.

From royalty such as the Duke of Edinburgh, sports stars like Trevor Brooking and Roger Black, musicians such as Acker Bilk and Chris Barber at the jazz nights at the Bull Hotel and Eypes Mouth, politicians Margaret Thatcher and Michael Foot, to acting and broadcasting stars such as Billie Whitelaw, Joss Ackland, David Jacobs and Rolf Harris.

Sometimes we found that the familiar friendly smiling outgoing star could be very sullen and uncooperative when away from the cameras and the crowd.

We respected the privacy of a Royal carpentry student when he was living in the area, only to be rewarded by him deliberately not turning up at an official press call.

Bill Harris and the Bridport News were very much involved with the revival of Bridport Carnival.

Photographing all the Miss Bridport and Mini Miss Bridport contestants made a lot of extra work every June.

The crowning ceremonies were often carried out in blustery conditions on a West Bay balcony by a star from the summer show at Weymouth.

It was also our privilege to be involved with local people, to share their celebrations such as to mark a diamond wedding or 100th birthday, to see the courage of a youngster like Simon Hill, or to watch a boy like Derek Walkey gradually progress from a primary school team to becoming a Bridport Football Club star.

There were dramatic scenes to photograph of runaway vehicles in Chideock and Charmouth, also upsetting events such as a young widow whose husband had met a tragic death, the poignant scene of a dog waiting vainly on the top of West Bay cliff after his master had committed suicide, and blood splattered vehicles at the site of fatal accidents.

Occasionally photographers from the national press would descend on the area and sometimes upset local people, leaving us to restore a good working relationship between press and public.

In the 1970s until the mid-1980s there was far more hospitality offered by organisations.

In those days we were often given tickets for dinners or entertainments but found understandably that as costs and overheads increased we usually ended up with just a coffee or a beer.

I wish today's digital cameras and computer technology had been available 20 years ago but I was very fond of my Pentax 67.

It would have saved so many rushed to print photographs taken late at night and then having to drive to Weymouth or Taunton so that they were available first thing for the block maker.

It was often difficult to convince a picture editor on a national paper that Weymouth was not just 10 minutes away with trains every half hour to get a photograph to London.

Maybe one of my most hurried jobs was when BBC television phoned about 1.30pm wanting photographs of some Bridport cottages involved in a demolition scheme.

Peter had gone to Dunkeswell to photograph a local pilot with her plane so I had to take and print the photographs.

Then, unable to get a courier or taxi, I drove to Plymouth in time for the pictures to be transmitted on the 6pm news. Through the late 1980s more newspapers employed staff photographers and we found ourselves mainly working for the Bridport News.

In 1991 Peter died suddenly and I decided to retire, having enjoyed my days in an originally unchosen career.

SEPTEMBER 1978

SOME tenants of two and three bedroomed council houses in West Dorset will be allowed to buy their properties, if a proposal put forward by Mr Ronald Coatsworth, who represents Bradpole on West Dorset District Council, is adopted by the authority.

Mr Coatsworth, of Beaumont Avenue, believes that the sale of council houses would be in the public interest.

MAY 1979

OVERWHELMING public objections to a proposal to close Bridport's Barrack Street to vehicular traffic have resulted in a county compromise to make the highway one-way for a six-month trial period.

JULY 1980

ON SCREEN and stage … written by Maureen Hymas.

In these fraught times there is nothing like a good belly laugh. How you get your laughs is another matter.

To some, Monty Python's Life of Brian (AA), which is a religious spoof, may be regarded as blasphemous.

To many critics it is richly funny, with all the silliness we have come to expect from the Python team.

Recommended only for the sight of John Cleese in Gladiator's rig!

It can be see at the Palace Cinema, Bridport, for seven days from Sunday.

JANUARY 1981

THERE was not a single protestor in sight when a colourful crowd of almost 2,000 turned up to greet the Cattistock Hunt at the traditional Boxing Day meet at Bridport.

The scene, depicting 'peace and goodwill' in its truest sense, was in stark contrast to some of recent years when anti-hunt demonstrators turned up in force to display placards decrying foxhunting as savage, cruel and barbaric.

MAY 1982

BRIDPORT is to have its first wine bar.

At Tuesday's Dorchester Crown Court Mrs Monique Stephens successfully appealed against Bridport licensing justices' refusal to grant her a provisional full 'on' licence for a wine bar at a former butcher's shop at 6, West Street.

Glamorous 70s with hamburger radios, go-fast stripes and platform shoes

APRIL 1983
A BRIDPORT man of Polish/Russian descent, whose early upbringing involved being shunted from country to country, received the British Empire Medal on Wednesday. Victor Seogalutze (33), of St Andrew's Road, an assistant inspector for the Bridport-Gundry subsidiary Bridport Aviation Products, received his award from the Lord Lieutenant of Dorset Col Sir Joseph Weld. During the Falklands crisis, Victor and his team gave up their spring holiday and worked all out to produce vital Ministry of Defence orders – specialised netting used by Chinook and Sea King helicopters.

JANUARY 1984
TOP disc jockey Steve Wright comes to Bridport on January 27, bringing his particular brand of zany humour to the Scruples nightspot in West Bay Road. Steve, probably Radio One's most popular personality, is the first in a line of top DJs the management of Scruples hope to bring to Bridport.

AUGUST 1985
RIGID plastic canopies over shops and other Bridport buildings were 'a passing fad like skateboards and yo-yos', said former Mayor Andy Bell.

JUNE 1986
BRIDPORT women will be taught how to beat off attackers at self-defence classes to be held in the town. The self-defence classes are the idea of Bridport Crime Prevention Panel, which is looking for an instructor to run the course. "It will not be a judo course for young, fit women, but basic self-defence tactics for women of all ages," said panel publicity officer, Mrs Christine Mears.

MAY 1987
DESIGN work on a replacement St Mary's School, at Bridport, has been approved by Dorset County Council's policy and support services sub-committee. Bridport county councillor Mike Smith said a substantial sum had been set aside to design the new school at Skilling Hill Road.

SEPTEMBER 1988
PLANS for a Regency-style mini-village within Bridport have been revealed this week. And, if town and district planners give the go-ahead, the development could give a new look to West Allington. Refine Design, the Bridport development company behind the scheme, wants to build 20 two-bedroomed 'cottage style' homes and 24 studio apartments on the former Bartletts store site.

By Steve Hunt
News reporter
1975-1978

I'D started my journalism training with my dad's news agency in Weymouth in 1974 and after a year or so I needed to get on to a newspaper to continue the course.

So I wrote, on his suggestion, to David Cozens, editor of the Bridport and Lyme Regis News, and was really pleased when he offered me a job as a cub reporter.

What I didn't know then was that in almost 30 years of journalism it would turn out to be one of the happiest times of my working life!

Seldom have I laughed so much, been so incredulous at day to day events or felt so much part of the gang.

I worked with the sort of larger than life characters who you seldom find in today's politically correct and, some would say, blander world of ours.

The staff line-up when I worked in Bridport comprised David Cozens, Philip Evans, Roger Bailey, Maureen Hymas and, latterly, Terry Collin.

I found early on that if you weren't actually involved in the 'incidents', you would certainly hear about them.

Roger Bailey, in particular, would relish the opportunity to tell and re-tell the best ones - and I, as a mere fresh-faced youth, was all ears.

Some were so extreme and unusual that you just knew they had to be true, and some definitely cannot be repeated here.

The risk of embarrassment and legal action would be too high. So I'll have to skip over the case of the exploding blow-up doll, along with the unpleasant stuffed pheasant affair.

Mind you, I can safely mention our canoeing reporter who nearly sank his own career when a search party sent out from the office spotted him paddling along the West Bay horizon. He should have been covering a meeting.

Then there was the keen job-seeker who walked into the editor's office for an interview with a live parrot on his shoulder. So I couldn't have joined the Bridport News at a better time – the office itself was a breeding ground for human interest stories, let alone those among the general Bridport and Lyme Regis populations.

On my first day David Cozens introduced me to the team – all very welcoming and I felt at home straight away.

When I walked in I seem to remember Roger and Maureen been engrossed in one of many conversations about her 'pussy'.

It seemed Maureen was something of a cat lover.

The first question fired at me was from Roger Bailey. He wanted to know the date and year of my birth. I thought it was for some official reason, but no.

It turned out that he would commit to memory every new recruit's birth details.

You could be in the middle of a conversation with him and he would suddenly break off and say, if it was me for instance: "April 11th, 1958."

Bit bizarre really, seeing as I already knew when I was born.

One of the traditions at the Bridport News in the 1970s was the mid-morning down tools for a cuppa at the West End Dairy.

And, likely as not, especially once the paper was virtually complete, an afternoon trog down to the Wimpy Bar.

It was in the Wimpy that a couple of my 'colleagues' hatched a plan to marry me off to the 16-year-old waitress who worked there every afternoon.

I know Philip Evans was involved, and possibly Maureen.

It must have caused great mirth and expectation among those in the know as the girl was called over to our table one afternoon.

HALCYON DAYS: Bridport News reporter Steve Hunt spent many happy days covering the news with the paper in the 1970s (SH)

BELOW LEFT: As he is today, a journalist and a pilot (SH)

I could only look on in increasing shock and embarrassment – I was only 17 and actually really fancied her but didn't have the guts to do anything about it – as Philip Evans proceeded to take on the role of a vicar at the table and announced the girl and I were to be married.

I remember protesting: "But I can't marry her – I haven't got a ring." At which point one of the 'guests' pushed across a large ring doughnut on a plate and said: "Use that."

I absolutely dread to think what the other customers made of it all.

And so, doughnut in hand, I asked my waitress to be my wife and, stunningly, she agreed.

Quite why the poor girl went along with it I don't know – either there had been a cash payment or something to do with my claim to fame at the same Wimpy Bar just a few weeks earlier.

Egged on (once again!) by my colleagues, I had reluctantly entered the regional Hamburger Radio Competition.

You had to say in 15 words why you wanted to win the first prize: namely, a transistor radio in the shape of a large plastic hamburger. Goodness knows how but I managed to win the competition and had my name put up on a contest poster in the Wimpy Bar.

Subsequently I was officially presented with my hamburger radio in a little ceremony at the Wimpy – that was OK, but frankly I could have done without the publicity in my own paper – someone wrote up the story and published it in the Bridport News.

Someone recently asked me if I still had that hamburger radio: no, I got rid of it pretty soon after.

It was really fiddly rotating the 'meat' bit, which doubled as the tuner. The radio also looked very silly and not something you'd exactly want to pull out in front of the girls.

Sadly, it wasn't the only time I made the news. I used to commute to Bridport from Weymouth along the coast road every day in my £130 Austin 1100 saloon.

It was 'racing' green and I had put DIY go-faster stripes up the bonnet using white insulating tape.

On Abbotsbury Hill, during one commute, the right front wheel and entire axle assembly and part of the gearbox parted company from the car.

Getting a wreck truck out and subsequent lift to the office was bad enough – even worse was the fact that half the people there knew all about it when I walked in.

The news information network was amazing in that area – and still is.

One thing was certain, there was no chance of keeping my 'accident' out of the paper.

And, as if to come back and haunt me, the News' 25 years ago column has featured both stories – the hamburger radio and Abbotsbury Hill fiasco, in recent years.

Sometimes, at lunchtime, I'd accompany Roger Bailey to the Bull for a pint.

One time it went on a bit longer, George the barman had even more tales to tell than usual.

Anyway, come 2.30pm and it's definitely time to leave – me, being a mere youth, slightly the worse for wear. In those days, in the heady 70s, I wore multi-coloured platform shoes with five-inch heels. I'd seen them in my nan's catalogue and thought they looked ace.

In my mad dash to leave the pub and get back to the office I slipped and my right heel broke clean off.

What was really weird was that although I looked everywhere, it seemed to have completely disappeared.

Basically it now meant I had to spend the afternoon wandering around the office, going out and interviewing people, and even covering a meeting, with a five-inch list. Unbelievably embarrassing. Again.

For some reason I seemed to have been sent out of the office more than usual that afternoon – no doubt to the great amusement of all.

That evening, and by now thoroughly fed up, I decided to go and have another look for my heel.

I was still paying off my shoes at £1 a week and faced having to fashion a new one of wood if I didn't find it.

What happened next is a tribute to the honesty of Bridport folk.

I walked into the Bull and, believe it or not, my heel was waiting for me behind the bar. Someone had actually handed it in!

OCTOBER 1989
SYMONDBSURY-based composer Andrew Dickson has gained the British Film Institute's award for his score of Mike Leigh's film, High Hopes.

AUGUST 1990
THE entire Bridport community breathed a mighty sigh of relief at the news that seven-year-old Gemma Lawrence had been rescued safe, and amazingly well, after a two-hour gun siege at her kidnapper's lair on West Bay's West Cliff. This followed probably the worst three days in the town's post-war history as residents and holidaymakers feared the worst for the little girl, snatched for her holiday park caravan during the early hours of Sunday morning.

APRIL 1991
A BRIDPORT man has been given a new heart and kidney in a single pioneering operation. Henry Smith, 48, of Lower Monkwood Farm, is only the second person in Britain to undergo the 'double' operation.

APRIL 1992
WEST Dorset Coroner Michael Johnston opened the inquest on Jo Ramsden yesterday and issued a grim warning: "It could be your child to be the next to go."

And he voiced an impassioned plea to help find the man who abducted Bridport woman Jo (21), whose remains were found in boggy woodland north of Lyme Regis last month.

FEBRUARY 1993
A CALL for urgent revitalisation of Bridport's commercial heart by the implementation of a town centre enhancement scheme is being made by business chief Richard Hindson.

As the new Leo's store in Sea Road North enters its third week of trading, shopkeepers are assessing the impact the supermarket is having on the town centre.

SEPTEMBER 1994
A VETERAN West Dorset farmer who has never owned a television set won the star prize in the Melplash Show draw – a portable TV. Father of five Henry Johnson (68), of Lower Ash Farm, Pymore, said: "What you don't have, you don't miss.

"We had a growing family and because there was no telly they found other things to do like crafts and outdoor activities."

JULY 1995

THE parish of Bradpole and Walditch has a woman priest. The Rev Maureen Allchin was officially welcomed into Bridport's team ministry by the Bishop of Sherborne.

She said: "Having a woman as their priest is new for many people but if I'm gentle and caring it will be overcome."

OCTOBER 1996

ALCOPOPS – controversial soft drinks laced with alcohol – are driving Bridport teenagers into bouts of vandalism which leave townsfolk to foot the bill, it was revealed this week.

Town councillors have backed a call from their finance and general purposes committee chairman Coun Bryan Wheeler and former mayor and local youth worker Phil Lathey for a community conference aimed at cracking down on a range of local drink-related public order problems.

MAY 1997

THE Bridport-Gundry group is finally ending its historic ties with the fishing industry with a cost of 30 jobs.

The company, from where ropes and cordage were once supplied to King John's navy, is making a third of the workforce redundant at its netmaking division over the next two months.

DECEMBER 1998

POLICE in Bridport look set to be operating from a new headquarters for the Millennium in a deal which will 'kick start' the controversial re-development of the town's run-down St Michael's Industrial Estate, the News can reveal.

West Dorset District Council agreed this week to co-operate in providing a site for the new local headquarters on land off Tannery Road, south of the Coach Station.

MARCH 1999

BBC chiefs say they will wait until the last moment to decide whether to commission a second series of Nick Berry's new TV show Harbour Lights.

A spokeswoman told The News this week that it would be 'an 11th hour decision' so that public reaction and viewing figures could be fully assessed.

The BBC's cautious approach comes after the show's first episode was panned by the critics – and got a lukewarm reception locally, despite universal acclaim for the West Dorset scenery.

Photographer RON BOSHIER received the call to arms after retiring with his wife Christine to Chideock following a photographic career spanning 40 years at the Basinstoke Gazette. Ron was a photographer on the Gazette and picture editor from 1948-1988. Ron came out of retirement to help the News and stayed for a decade. Here he tells his story ...

START OF SOMETHING BIG: Ron and his wife Chris soak up the sun in Barbados, reading the Bridport News, now a regular feature the weekly paper (RB)

Ron came out of his retirement to bowl 'em over

RETIREMENT in this delightful Area of Outstanding Natural Beauty meant time to go fishing and daily walk the dog on the Jurassic coastline, usually finishing at the Anchor Inn, Seatown, and with time to ramble the unspoilt countryside.

In August 1991 I received a phone call from Gazette chairman Mr Alan Jones asking me if I could help the local paper, the Bridport News, by taking some photographs for them. News freelance photographer Peter Payne had sadly passed away and left the paper short of a photographer to cover the weekend work. I told them I would be pleased to help them out but unfortunately I had sold all my professional equipment and only kept a single lens Canon camera.

One of my first weekend assignments was to cover a cricket match at the village of Melplash where the home team was in action against a team from Verwood. When I arrived at the charming village ground surrounded by cornfields almost touching the boundary on one side and the local pub the Half Moon on the other side, I met the Melplash captain Peter Marks. I explained my camera problem of not having any long lenses to get good action pictures of the match.

Peter said not to worry, as the News usually did a large team photograph and a small picture of the opening batsman. I suggested that if the umpire and other team agreed, I could stand inside the boundary and get nearer the action for the first few balls. I might get a reasonable action shot.

A delighted Peter returned and said everyone had agreed to my request. He had won the toss and Melplash would bat first. Peter opened for Melplash and was happy for me to stand in close for his opening overs. Unfortunately for the Melplash skipper, he was bowled out with good ball that sent the bails flying and gave me a good action shot.

Bridport News sports editor Terry Collin liked my photograph of the Melplash skipper's dismissal and used a large, five-column picture across the top of the sports page with a headline 'Timber'.

Peter was not very happy when the Bridport News came out and said the picture and headline had caused a lot of comment – I replied that it had also generated a lot of publicity for Melplash Cricket Club. I enjoyed many visits to Melplash Cricket Ground with my new Nikon and 300mm and 600mm lenses I captured good pictures of Peter and his team hitting fours and sixes into the corn fields.

There were many good evenings in the popular Half Moon public house where the club held its annual presentation dinners, where Fido would always be found. (Fido May is the club's president. For 18 months, the news ran a weekly competition to find Fido's head, hidden somewhere in the paper).

I finished my weekend help and handed in my sports and news photographs. To my surprise, I carried on helping for the next ten years of my retirement.

Ten enjoyable years taking photographs in this delightful patch of Dorset, covering Bridport, Beaminster, Lyme Regis and all the charming villages like Chideock.

Plenty of good photographic opportunities covering carnivals, Melplash Show, West Bay raft and trawler races and all the fetes,

GREAT START: Photographer Ron Boshier captures the moment on his first job for the Bridport News when Melplash captain and opener Peter Marks is bowled out (RB)

flower shows plus a good selection of sport. Making many good friends with Bridport News and Weymouth Echo staff and dozens of Dorset friends at all the interesting assignments.

In the early days all the photographs were black and white in the Bridport News. With no dark room, I had to turn my garden shed into one. I spent most of my Sunday evenings printing my weekend sport and news photographs, then taking over my wife's kitchen to wash and dry the prints.

Life got easier when we shot everything in colour. I would drop my colour films through Boots letter box on Sundays and my prints were finished Monday morning, ready for collection.

The colour pictures made a great improvement to the paper, bringing extra life to the photographs, especially the carnivals, fetes and shows.

Spending a wet Saturday afternoon at St Marys Field with Terry Collin covering a Bridport FC match, when a good colour sports picture on the sports page of the Bees' winning goal brightened a wet Saturday.

In June, 2000, my wife and I celebrated our Golden Wedding with a cruise from Barbados to Rio de Janeiro to see the spectacular Millennium Rio Carnival with its 20,000 colourful performers.

News editor Margery Hookings wanted to start a new feature with readers sending in photographs of themselves reading the Bridport News in interesting, exotic locations.

To start the feature I submitted a picture of us reading the News with a front page headline "Celebrating a Special Day", on our golden "special day" in the Barbados sunshine. The feature became very popular, with readers sending in photographs from all over the world.

The Chideock Society decided to produce a Millennium commemorative book, A Wander Through Chideock, looking at the past, the present and the future of the village. For the past, the locals searched through cupboards, in attics and blew the dust off old photo albums.

For the present, I photographed a series of colour views around the village and a selection of my photographs that had been published in the Bridport News.

Pictures of local personalities, Professor Denys Brunsden, international expert inspecting the Jurassic Coast at Seatown, Dave Symonds, thatcher, working his 1908 thrashing machine, Kathleen Symes, the long serving postmistress's retirement, Chideock cidermakers trying a new brew in the cider shed. Children of Chideock photographed what parts of the village they would like to see kept for them to enjoy in the future, playground, sweet shops, church and the local pubs featured in their selected photographs.

Photography and cameras have taken a huge technical leap forward since I started my photographic career. My first press assignment was photographing the Reading cricket team with a 10x8 brass and mahogany plate camera, complete with a black focusing clothing, but no shutter only a lens cap.

Then came the 5x4 Micro-Press camera complete with a flash gun and a bag of flash bulbs, then 2 / square roll film before 35mm cameras and I became a Nikon man.

Today, with digital cameras, laptop processors and portable photoprinters it makes a press photographer's job much easier and quicker for the picture desk.

With roads closed, Bridport town centre became a huge party on New Year's Eve. Most people in colourful fancy dress and in merry high spirits.

My favourite spot to get good photographs of the fun was to balance on top of the railings under the town hall.

One year, precariously balancing on the railings, holding on with one hand and camera in the other, a large, brown, female 'bear' attacked me.

In a flash, my trousers were down around my ankles before I could climb down from the town hall railings.

I got a good page of fun pictures of the fancy dress revellers but luckily no one got the best picture of the evening.

ON THE WILD SIDE: Ron's favourite walk is to Golden Cap with his golden retriever Giles, finishing at the Anchor pub at Seatown (RB)

APRIL 2000
DRUG addicts in the Bridport area are shoplifting to finance their habit. In the last 12 months, there have been 91 shoplifting offences compared with 44 in the previous year. Section commander Inspector Tim Warren said: "Shoplifting is mainly drug-related and we're talking about addictive drugs such as heroin."

JUNE 2001
A SECOND wave of illegal immigrants have been caught in Dorset. A man and a woman were found hiding in a lorry container on the North Mills Trading Estate in Bridport. The container had travelled from Italy. The discovery follows a major operation by police and immigration officers to trap a yacht full of illegal immigrants in Weymouth.

SEPTEMBER 2002
A PUBLIC meeting is being held in Bridport tonight in response to a supermarket's plans to expand its services. Safeway says up to 50 new jobs will be created by the scheme which includes a new café, a photo development area, dry cleaners and more leisure products. But campaigners fear the development will have an adverse effect on the area and are questioning the impact it will have on other businesses, the town centre and the wider area.

OCTOBER 2003
BRIDPORT'S stature as a centre for food excellence is continuing to grow.

Next week, prime minister Tony Blair will congratulate the West Dorset Food and Land Trust for the part it has played in the promotion of local food.

The accolade comes just months after Bridport was awarded beacon town status by the Countryside Agency in recognition of the area's thriving food sector and the work of the trust to promote local food.

MAY 2004
A NEW organisation is being set up in Bridport to tackle the affordable housing crisis. The Bridport Community Property Trust will work with other groups by providing the structure for low-cost homes to become a reality. It is an offshoot of the successful West Dorset Food and Land Trust.

MAY 2005
PLANS for West Bay's multi-million pound facelift are finally going on public display. Detailed drawings of the proposed regeneration scheme will be unveiled by the district council on Monday, launching the long-awaited next round of public consultation.

The kidnap of little Gemma, 7

ON the morning of Sunday, August 12, 1990, I was woken by a ringing telephone.

The caller, who I knew well, suggested I quickly get down to West Bay as a real-life drama was unfolding.

Just hours earlier, at 4.30am, little Gemma Lawrence, a seven-year-old on holiday with her parents at the Haven site, had been abducted from her caravan.

For the next two days, it seemed all hell had broken loose in Bridport. The town and the Bay were full of police, and the 'rat pack' from Fleet Street.

There was extreme concern for Gemma's safety. Coastguards and soldiers joined with hundreds of holidaymakers and residents to scour the area as the Royal Naval helicopter from Portland searched the cliffs.

It was a nightmare happening in Bridport. The Dorset Evening Echo, for which I was then working as a district reporter, put out two editions as we were given a special daily press conference by the head of Dorset CID.

The police's main priority was to find Gemma and catch the man who had taken her. The local paper was seen as vital in assisting in that search.

On Tuesday lunchtime, I remember being just about to interview the police chief on the steps of Bridport Police Station, then in St Andrew's Road, when an officer came along, whispered in his ear and he hurried away.

Not long afterwards, I drove down to the Bay where I saw a police car with a man in the back, blanket over his head, being driven away.

Gemma Lawrence was safe and well. She had been kept imprisoned in the garden shed of a derelict chalet bungalow, a short distance from the family's caravan.

She was released after an armed siege of the property, where drifter Paul Burton, 23, from Sussex, had made a secret hideout.

The relief felt by townsfolk was almost palpable but there was disquiet when it was realised police and volunteers had searched the area near the kidnapper's lair within hours of her abduction.

The main thing, however, was that Gemma was alive.

In February, 1991, Paul Burton, described in Winchester Crown Court as 'an unfortunate, tormented creature' was sent to Broadmoor without any time limit.

LEFT: Margery Hookings today and right as she looked in 1991 (JG)

Punk whose day was made by the News

By Margery Hookings
Bridport News editor 1999-2004

WHEN I first joined the Bridport News in 1982, I was already in awe of sports editor Roger Bailey and I hadn't even met him.

I remember being interviewed at the offices of the Somerset County Gazette in Taunton by the then editor David Cozens.

It was about the time of the Falklands War and I was just about to finish my journalism training.

I was amazed to be offered the job as I had spiky red hair, drainpipe jeans and monkey boots. I am told it was quite a shock for Bridport, where 20-somethings all had perms and big collars.

But David Cozens told me at the end of the interview I had been successful (I think I was probably the only applicant).

He then proceeded to fill me in on the rest of the staff.

There was Terry Collin and eternal teenager Maureen Hymas. There was fellow 'youngster' Paul James, with his Dr Who scarf and quick wit.

There was freelance photographer Peter Payne and his wife Mary.

"And then there's Roger Bailey," he said. Unusually for Dave, he was lost for words in how to

Jo tragedy touched everyone

JUST months after Gemma Lawrence's kidnapper was sent to Broadmoor, 21-year-old Jo Ramsden went missing while on her way to Bridport Leisure Centre in April, 1991.

Troops joined police and volunteers in combing the fields for clues as helicopters conducted a search from the skies. Divers probed the murky waters of the River Brit and West Bay harbour.

But although sparking off one of the biggest police inquiries to be mounted in Dorset, the case did not initially attract the same level of national publicity as Gemma's disappearance.

Jo, who attended Bridport Adult Training Centre and helped out at her parents' gift shop, had Down's Syndrome.

Her story was overshadowed by the disappearance of an attractive university student that happened at around the same time.

Mencap leader Lord Rix and Sir James Spicer, then West Dorset's MP, presented a huge petition to the BBC for publicity. A reconstruction on Crimewatch triggered more than 600 calls but to no avail.

For nearly a year, her parents hoped against hope that their only daughter would turn up safe. The couple's quiet dignity touched everyone and it was a town in mourning when Jo's remains were discovered in woodland north of Lyme Regis in March, 1992.

Just over a year later, a judge at Cardiff Crown Court ruled there was insufficient evidence to try Michael Fox, 49, from Charminster, on the charge of abducting Jo. It was a charge he had consistently denied.

Fox, admitted five counts of kidnapping other mentally handicapped women, three of rape and one of attempted rape and asked for nine other offences to be taken into consideration.

Mr Justice McKinnon ordered the charge of abducting Jo should lie on file. Dorset Police said they would not look for anyone else in connection with her death.

Fox, a former psychiatric nurse, was given nine life sentences and ended up in Broadmoor.

The town's then rector, the Rev John Gann, said: "Jo was one of our people who was taken right in the midst of us. Her abduction illustrated the sad and evil effects in modern life. In a strange way, a lot of good came out from the community when it happened. We saw the best side and also had the horrible reminder of what modern life is like, which perhaps we are a bit shielded from in this area."

NEWS MAKERS: The reporting team at the Bridport News in 2003. From the left, Sarah Thompson, Chris Carson, Margery Hookings, photographer John Gurd, Rene Gerryts, Rosemary Lewis and Lisa Youd (MH)

describe Roger. He just said: "Don't worry, he's harmless. You'll get used to him."

I arrived in Bridport the weekend before I was due to start. I'd only ever been to Bridport once, even though I was born and brought up less than 20 miles away.

It was a love affair that has lasted ever since.

It was a windswept Sunday and I was on top of the East Cliff at West Bay. This was a place I could settle in.

The next day, I arrived at the ramshackle office in East Street – in those days, both advertising and editorial were crammed on to the ground floor.

I was introduced to my new colleagues. I got to Roger and naively said: "Oh yes, I've heard all about you."

"Whaddya bluddy mean?" he said, pointing his finger.

I shook my head rapidly and stuttered: "Uh, uh, Dave's told me all about you."

"Has he indeed?"

My heart sank.

Roger was a big man, with big features and huge great hands. He had the voice of brown Windsor soup and swayed from side to side when he walked, his Express tucked under one arm and a Happy Shopper plastic carrier bag swinging from the other.

He and Maureen Hymas, a senior reporter whom I envied because she also used to write the film column, made those early days of my career something to write home about.

I have never been able to take anything, least of all myself, very seriously since.

Roger had this amazing habit of remembering everyone's date of birth, even strangers in the street, and reciting it at them, finishing off with 'twig it'?

He could also belch 'Burt Boulton' and 'happy birthday to you' – a feat I have always admired.

Roger had a wonderful singing voice and Maureen and I would constantly badger him to sing 'Animal Crackers'.

He also was reputed to have the largest, how shall I say it? Ahem, tackle in West Dorset.

This has since been confirmed by two people, independently of each other.

I was told by one contemporary that as a young man, Roger was bowling at cricket when his trousers ripped and his undercarriage worked loose.

Every game thereafter, dozens of girls would be among the spectators, hoping for a repeat performance. Another who remembers Roger from his umpiring days, recalls a story about a particularly over-confident young cricketer from an opposing side who was particularly proud of his own manhood.

He went into the toilets and was alongside Roger at the urinals. When he came out, the player was a gibbering wreck and insisted on calling Roger 'sir' all through the game.

With the editor David Cozens and Terry Collin safely ensconced in another office, Maureen and I would egg Roger on to do the most outrageous things, like walking across to George's Bakery with a sign on his back saying 'Stop Me and Try One' or 'Proud Stallion'. We once made a nurse's paper hat with a red cross on it and dared Roger to go down the West End Dairy wearing it.

Of course he always did.

We would frequently get visitors in the office, many of whom would just come in for a chat. Invariably, Maureen would dive under her desk and hide out the way, leaving the young junior (me) to deal with them.

It was usually me that ended up talking to a local character, Jack Hutchings, an old beret-wearing gentleman who used to ride up on his bike from his South Street home. "I want you to write a letter

A privilege to serve the community

for me," he would say. When Maureen drew the short straw, she would take down his comments and turn them into the most eloquent pieces of writing I had ever seen..

Albert Cast (the father of Keith, the artist) was another frequent visitor. He lived next door and used to come in to the News by the side door.

Waving his walking stick at Roger, who was listening to the cricket on the radio, he'd say: "What's the score Rog?"

Maureen, meanwhile, had dived for cover under the desk having heard Albert shuffling up the corridor.

She would let out the occasional woof or miaow to which Roger would take great delight in saying: "There's a pussy in here Albert." It was around the time of Are You Being Served when Mrs Slocombe's pussy had become a national institution.

Poor old Albert – but I think he was actually in on the joke.

Jack and Albert – and there was also Frank Willett from West Bay who wore slippers, had no teeth, and drove a light blue Reliant Robin – were actually welcome diversions from the daily grind.

Working on a local newspaper was jolly hard work. Endless council meetings, tedious although occasionally juicy court cases that went on into the early evenings and some weekend work involving fetes and ferret racing.

What people didn't realise was that we didn't get time off in lieu for all those extra hours.

There were good stories and there were sad ones, there were stories about oversized vegetables and people who tripped over paving slabs.

Stories that stick out in my mind include the court case where the magistrates had to adjourn and hold a session in the gents' toilets in King Street after hearing evidence from a police officer.

The toilets had been kept under observation and the officer claimed to have witnessed a lewd act as he

REPORTER'S FEET: Former News reporter Paula Roberts looks at Roger Bailey's footprints underneath the desk he sat at for many years at the East Street office (CC)

looked under the door of a cubicle. The defendant's solicitor said he couldn't have seen anything from that angle.

The magistrates duly trooped down to the toilets and tested the viewpoint out for themselves.

The defendant was convicted.

I also remember being in court when the magistrates retired to discuss some legal point or other with the clerk.

It was just me, the defendant, his wimpish solicitor and a detective left in the court room.

Suddenly, the defendant lunged towards the detective, ramming him up against the door. He held the policeman up by the throat and, among the obscenities, I caught the words: "You've been sleeping with my girlfriend." The police inspector the other side of the door pleaded with the defendant to stop, the solicitor was almost as petrified as I was, and then everything calmed down. The magistrates came back in, none the wiser about this unusual outburst.

I always think my best story was one about a young disabled man who lived with his parents in their council house. Under the right to buy scheme, everyone around them were buying their homes. But because part of their house had been adapted for their son, they were not allowed to.

I got to hear about the situation and the resulting story led to the council taking a vote and changing the rules.

My most vivid memory is of a meeting at St Mary's Church when Mountjoy School was facing closure. There were about 400 people there and one after another, they got up and told the bemused bureaucrats what they thought of their plans.

It was an emotional moment helped, I think, by the quiet but determined campaign run by the Bridport News to save Mountjoy School.

The school is still there and so are the pupils but, every now and then, a story emerges which reveals they are still facing an uncertain future.

An easily accessible newspaper office in the heart of the town is great for good local stories. But it also attracts the occasional lunatic, who will not leave unless you listen to this bizarre tale of woe and promise to put it in the paper for them.

Like the man with strange glasses (I swear there were eyes painted on the outside) who insisted we do a story on him.

"My neighbours are harassing me," he said.

"Why's that?" I said.

"I don't know but they're persecuting me because of my beliefs."

"And what are they?"

"Paganism and the Irish Republican Army."

"That'd be it then," I said.

Having said I would not be doing a story on him, he came back, arguing at the top of his voice that he was going to report me to the Press Council for not publicising his plight.

Then there are the people up on assault charges at court. You can guarantee that when you carry a report of the court case, the defendant or his mother will turn up threatening to duff you up if you write about it again.

You're at the heart of the community and when you report something, however accurate, it's always the messenger that gets it when people don't like the news.

Like the time I came under siege by a councillor for daring to let people have their say in the newspaper when they felt that Framptons the butchers was threatened by plans to revamp the Town Hall.

"You know your problem?" he said. "You think you're up there and we're down here."

That was shortly after taking over as editor of the paper I first joined at the tender age of 20.

Being at the helm of a small country newspaper, in a town like Bridport, had its ups and downs – but it was an absolute privilege to be at the heart of such a special community, reporting on its comings and goings.

I still can't walk down the street without seeing someone I know some story about. That's the man who ran off with the woman who had the dog that bit the postman who nicked the letters … and on and on. It's like there's a running commentary in my head. Priceless.

They seek him here, they seek him there

GAME FOR A LAUGH: Fido May featured in the News' weekly competition Find Fido where readers had to scour the paper to spot one of Bridport's most colourful characters (MH)

FIND FIDO was a weekly just-for-fun competition that seemed to sum up the quirky side of Bridport.

Each week, his face was planted somewhere in the paper. Readers rang in to complain if he was missing.

The feature centred on Fido May, who has become a familiar face as parade marshall at the Remembrance Day marches.

He is also a key figure in the local Royal National Lifeboat Institution and Royal British Legion.

Originally, the plan was to hide a specially created cartoon character in the paper – children born in the 60s may remember Baby Moonbeam in the Pippin comics. The editor was looking for something similar that summed up the area.

And then someone said: "That Fido May's in everything." From that point, a scheme was hatched to Find Fido. Mr May was invited to a local pub for a soft drink and the mysterious words: "There's something I would like to discuss with you."

When the plan was unveiled, he took it well and good-heartedly agreed to participate.

For a short time, Find Fido became a local institution, although it backfired one week when his head was substituted for someone else's in a crowded running picture. It was thought there was no way the person concerned would be able to make out himself, because he was right at the back.

But the owner of the body rang to ask why his head was not his own, having first seen the picture in the Dorset Echo.

Writers rattled cages and filled postbags

FOR more than 40 years, The Wanderer has been making contributions to the Bridport News.

Originally a diary section compiled by former editor Foxy Harris, it contained snippets of news from around the area.

It then became a page to which all the reporters contributed.

In the 1990s, former town crier Harry Poole, a retired farmer, became the man in the street and wrote a weekly column of things he had heard round and about the town.

In recent years, a new Wanderer, Barkins, made his mark. In the short time the column existed, the Wanderer rattled a few cages and got people either really worked up and angry or nodding their heads in agreement.

His pieces resulted in bumper postbags, with many readers desperate to know the author's identity.

This was someone who knew the town really well, and had done for some time. He was not afraid to say what he thought and would not suffer fools gladly.

But The Wanderer was actually two people – a man and a woman.

To this day, only a handful of people know their identity.

Music master left his mark on thousands

BRIDPORT has long been a magnet for creative people.

But the town can be justly proud of its home grown talent, particularly those who have been influenced by the 'Rex' factor.

Rex Trevett, who died in 2005, literally made his mark on thousands of people. There were those taught by him when he was head of music at Colfox School and those who listened to his incredible music-making and that of his students.

Rex was self-taught, a hairdresser by trade but a musician at heart, even though an early school report suggested he had no musical ability.

Jazz was Rex's forte and his Colfox Big Band days were among the happiest of his life. And for years, he was the man at the helm of the town band, St Swithun's. Music was his great love and his legacy lives on in those who chose it as a career – like saxophonist Mike Smith, pianist Dan Dibdin and rock diva Polly Harvey – and others who enjoy it as a hobby.

From plush offices to seat cushions in the window!

By Sarah Thompson

Bridport News reporter 2001-2005

THE brown and yellow window seat cushions struck me first, then the Hessian carpet.

It was not how I had expected a newsroom to look like at all.

I had left my job at one of London's biggest marketing agencies where I worked on the sixth floor of a glass-fronted building.

People in expensive suits whizzed up and down in glass lifts and had conference calls in breakfast meetings.

Walking up the emergency steps at the back of the Bridport News into the uneven and cramped office with the brown and yellow window seats cushions (what office has window seats, let alone cushions?), I wondered what I had let myself in for.

But all memories of business meetings and power lunches would soon fade as the rollercoaster ride of local news and the team at the Bridport office became my world.

I joined the news as a trainee in September 2001.

It was part of my contract that I would go to a journalism training college in Darlington in the following February, and until then I would do all the usual stuff a junior reporter does.

During my first week a man came in clutching a giant 3lb carrot that he had grown 'by accident' in his back garden.

Having always lived in the city, where the local papers mostly reported crime and more crime, I was amazed that people would bother to bring in their giant vegetables.

As I stood outside the office watching photographer John Gurd take a picture of the man with his enormous root vegetable, I realised this was probably one of the best jobs in the world.

I wrote a caption that said: "This is a turnip for the books ... well, it's a carrot actually."

When the editor, Margery, laughed and didn't insist write something less stupid, I knew it was going to be fun working with her.

The ridiculousness of the carrot episode was juxtaposed the following week with one of the biggest disasters the world has ever seen – 9/11.

Chris Carson took a call from the Lyme Regis photographer Richard Austin, who said there had been some sort of accident at the World Trade Centre.

We watched with horror – as did the rest of the world – as the truth unfolded. The News discovered that two Bridport people had been killed in the attack but the News took the decision to keep our reporting on them low-key, out of respect for the families of those involved.

It was in contrast to how other local papers treated their tragic news, and I remember being pleased to be part of a paper that was truly for local people and not just about the headlines that sold most papers.

Over the next few months I covered stories ranging from flower shows and golden wedding anniversaries to exploding fridges and women drivers caught wearing oven gloves.

I had always considered myself a fairly worldly sort of girl. I had grown up in Birmingham and lived and worked in London for eight years. Yet my first few months as a reporter in Bridport taught me there was still a lot to learn about life.

I quickly developed a taste for feature writing, it gave me the chance to use my flair and I enjoyed the interviews as they usually meant going out of the office.

As the rookie who was still full of enthusiasm and wonder at this fantastic job I'd landed, the rest of the guys were happy to let me have the free para-gliding lesson or to try the Dances of Universal Peace at Monkton Wyld.

I even got to have my nails painted and then to write about it.

One job I'll never forget was meeting the Chideock Cider Makers in their old shed.

I was feeling a bit low that Tuesday evening in October and didn't really want to trudge all the way to some old shack in Chideock to meet a bunch of old cider-heads.

It turned out to be one of the loveliest evenings I'd ever had and was the beginning of a friendship with the group, who are tireless fundraisers and some of the funniest and most genuine people I've ever met.

(When I asked, in all seriousness, at what point did they add the alcohol, they didn't laugh at me half as hard as they could have.)

After six months I went off to Darlington in Northumbria for a 20-week training course with 16 other journalists from all over the country.

Four hours of shorthand a day and a gruelling schedule of law and public affairs classes during the freezing cold winter meant I was often in tears and wishing I could be back home.

But looking back I realise how much I achieved and how much fun I had. I also made friends for life and can now boast of knowing journalists all over the world.

Back at the News I settled into my job and began to get to know my colleagues better.

I shared the lower office (the one with the window seats) with Chris Carson and Rene Gerryts, both of them experienced journalists.

Chris always made me laugh with his quiet humour.

He always did a little startled jump when ever his phone rang, as if he didn't know that's what they did.

Chris liked to claim that he wasn't a people person but he had a way with everyone he met and could always get people to tell their story, perhaps because he never pressurised them.

He wrote the best, sharpest news copy in the office and had a real talent for funny picture captions and puns.

I would often be writing a picture caption and turn to Chris and say: "What can I write for this bus picture Chris?" And quick as anything he'd reply: "Just the ticket, hold tight, ding-dong…..?"

He had a 'funny' for every situation.

When talking to someone on the phone he would type his notes (rather than write them in a notebook) and so the click-clacking of Chris's keyboard became the soundtrack to the working day.

He was also very patient and rarely lost his rag when dealing with awkward people or when the office computers went down, which they did with alarming regularity.

He was perhaps the most patient, however, when forced to listen to the endless chit-chat that went on between Rene and me.

Rene had a melodic voice that went up and down like a song and she talked really quickly, often telling you something, followed by a joke and a burst of laughter, all before you had a chance to think of anything to say.

That's why she was such a good journalist and feature writer especially – she was a natural story teller.

Never short of words, or observations, she could keep you entertained for hours with tales of her life on the farm and her horses.

And she always lent great emotion to whatever it was she was talking about, which was why you wanted to listen.

Poor Chris would sit quietly in the middle as we discussed men with their myriad faults and the mysteries of the menstrual cycle. I could sense his anguish as we swapped bra catalogues and discussed the strangely appealing gruffness of Richard Austin over a biscuit.

Chris became an honorary member of our unofficial diet club and would really try to be nice about it when I came in from lunch proudly displaying a new pair of shoes or coat from the charity shop.

During all this chat, however, Rene would be typing away and bashed out twice the amount of stories I could manage in a week.

She always gave the impression of being slightly disorganised and a bit hectic but underneath it all she knew what she was doing.

BOWING OUT: Former Bridport News reporter Mike Hannon who is now living the life of Riley in France (RB)

Margery was the one who had faith in me and took me on when I had no journalistic experience, so I was always grateful and slightly in awe of her.

Like all good bosses, she kept a slight detachment from the rest of us and you always felt there was a lot more to know about her than she let on.

Looking back it was probably because she was working so hard.

She was a hands-on editor and her byline was up there with everyone else's week after week.

And she was impressive to watch. She knew absolutely everyone and always found out about the gossip, even if some of it couldn't be printed.

Being a local she had a real sense of what people wanted to read and tapped in to the quirky and slightly off-the-wall personality of Bridport with the features and news stories she chose. (My peers at journalism college couldn't believe that we had a game called Find Fido, in which readers were invited to find the head of RNLI boss Fido May every week, just for fun – it was usually on someone's bum or driving in a car).

She knew what each of us was good at and was happy to let us indulge our interests as long as it made good copy.

Where else could I have written a feature about De Vinchies nightclub? (John Gurd the photographer loved doing that piece as he got to take pictures of semi-clad women dancing. I loved it as I got to drink pints of lager all in the name of research.)

Friday mornings were always my favourite part of the week as we all sat with a cup of tea and went through the freshly printed paper. There would always be some sort of mistake that made us laugh.

Like the time all our surnames were left off our bylines, so the front page story was 'By Margery' and the back page 'By Chris' and so on.

While most of these were funny, there would sometimes be a more serious mistake, or someone would take umbrage at a story.

Margery was always fiercely protective of her staff and I can recall her defending me on a number of occasions when I had upset someone or other.

Like the then curator of the Bridport museum who was most indignant when I wrote in my profile of her that she was six feet tall (she was actually around five foot eight, I can be prone to exaggeration), had long blond hair and was far too attractive for the job.

She said her friends had read it and thought I fancied her. (I didn't, by the way).

After a while Margery gave me the Lyme Regis edition to handle on my own and I soon became immersed in the news and views of people in Lyme Regis.

A whole book could be written about the in-fighting and scandals of that pretty little town.

It is a curious place, cut off from the rest of the world by the sea on one side and an enormous hill on the other.

Displaced from the rest of West Dorset, it is far away from its own governing district council and in constant battle with neighbouring East Devon.

Its secluded way of life is under constant threat from the barrage of retirees and second homers who, albeit unintentionally, suck the lifeblood from the very town they love so much.

As a result it is a town where the indigenous tribes do daily battle with the Surrey set whose second homes drive up the house prices and fill the high street with nice but expensive shops.

Many of the key councillors in the town have been in office for decades, and I especially enjoyed watching and reporting the interaction between this band of brothers.

All this makes for great stories of course and it's hard to imagine a village anywhere else (for with a population of that size, Lyme is smaller than many villages) having a paper that is read so vociferously by so many.

The letters page was often full of hilarious, incredible and at times downright spiteful sentiments.

So, while working on the Bridport News was an education and an eye-opener, being the Lyme Regis News reporter was a baptism of fire and in the truest sense I feel that now I can cope with anything.

AT YOUR SERVICE: The advertising team at the Bridport News in 2005. Left to right, Helen Dommett, Lisa Baker, Fran Stanford and Nicola Mann

(BN)

Man of extraordinary talent

ONE of Bridport's biggest success stories is artist Keith Cast, whose paintings are in collections all over the world.

For a spell, there was even one of Keith's pictures on a wall in Coronation Street.

He has a passion for the area that is understandable to those of us that live here.

His depictions of the West Dorset coast and countryside are very traditional. They may not be to everyone's taste, particularly those with a penchant for unmade beds and a wall of bricks, the things that these days pass for modern art.

But people like his work. You can see what they are and, if you know the area, where they are, even though he uses artistic licence when appropriate.

He is scathing about modern art, believing his artist's palette, with its vibrant mix of colours, could be framed and successfully exhibited alongside some of the work at the Tate. Keith was born in West Bay in October, 1927. He has had little formal art tuition and his interest in painting began in 1946 when he was serving in the RAF in Sudan.

He left school at 14, destined for a variety of jobs, including ones with Bridport gasworks, the electricity board, projectionist at the Lyric and Palace cinemas and a farm worker.

One of the lovely things about Keith is his ordinariness. He is a Bridport man through and through, completely unaffected, not pretentious by any stretch of the imagination but blessed with a gift few of us will ever personally experience.

He may have been born with a natural talent for art but the road to success has been a long haul.

"It's mainly due to determination," he says.

"There is no quick fix. Today, many budding artists' attitude to success is how quick they can complete a picture and to take advantage of all the promotional grants that can be obtained.

"It takes years of determination. I have never had any grants of any kind but in the early days I had to work at other jobs and paint in my spare time.

"There is also a slight element of luck, being in the right place at the right time."

Paper helps play important role in West Dorset life

By Holly Robinson
Bridport News editor from 2004

LOOKING AHEAD: Holly Robinson became the latest editor of the Bridport News in 2004 (BN)

AS communities change so do the newspapers that record the comings and goings of the people who live in the towns and villages they serve.

Throughout the last 150 years the Bridport News has been there diligently recording life in West Dorset, amassing a fascinating chronicle of the county's history.

Tales of war efforts at home and abroad, storms, elections, village and town events, agriculture, industry, schools, local government activities and health issues are among the subjects regularly featured in the pages of the News.

Many of these issues arise time and again, decade after decade, as can be seen by our popular weekly feature looking back into our files from 100, 75, 50 and 25 years ago.

Whether it is traffic congestion, coastal defence works, new housing, or problems, or successes, in our hospitals and schools, some things never change.

The News has an important part to play in the life of West Dorset's towns and villages, a fact never underestimated by the dedicated staff of journalists and advertising executives who work to bring out the newspaper each Friday.

Of course newspapers evolve as technology does. Over the years advances have allowed more pages and more colour pictures and adverts, and better access to reporters with the advent of mobile phones and email. A look through the files also shows how trends change along the way, with cosmetic tweaks to fonts and design reflecting the era the paper was published as well as the practicalities of the printing press of the day.

The heart and soul of any newspaper is fed by its readers and the comings and goings of their lives. Without readers the newspaper would not exist and local papers must put together the right package of news, information, and campaigns.

Reporters must write about the issues people care about and expect to read as well as passing on those snippets of information and jaw dropping nuggets people can only rely on their newspaper to dig up.

The local newspaper is the first thing turned to for what's-on information, entertainment and leisure ideas, details of homes and cars for sale, tide tables, pictures of events and activities, local campaigns and fundraising, and the latest local authority decisions.

We are there to record life and death, ups and downs, and the complicated changes to local authorities and public health bodies that will have an affect on readers' lives. But we are also there to record the wacky, lighter hearted side of life.

When our reporters attend meetings or court sessions and when they ask questions about events in our towns and villages, they are acting as the eyes and ears of the public.

But we are also there to give readers a voice – whether it is through a story or our lively letters page where people can have their say on all manner of subjects - where they otherwise may not have one.

Technological advances now mean stories and pictures whizz down the line to our production department at Weymouth and the printing press, but these days the newspaper could be printed anywhere in the UK or even abroad.

For a community newspaper to be successful it is vital to have 'newshounds' on the ground and reporters are encouraged to go out and about in their patch digging up stories to see what is going on. The News' strength lies in its relationship with its readers. A constant flow of people pop into the office or call up reporters to pass on snippets of information or suggest issues the team may want to look into.

As for the future, yes there will be changes along the way, with new faces and the odd tweak here and there, but our fundamental aim will always be the same. We strive to deliver local news and information our readers can trust, and to champion issues that strike at the very heart of the communities we serve.

It just remains to say a big thank you to all our readers who loyally pick up the 'Wip Wop' each week and we look forward to bringing you the next 150 years of Bridport and Lyme Regis News.

The day when Alison stopped the press

WEST Dorset woman Alison MacDermott remembers one of her greatest moments – the day she got the presses stopped just after the paper was put to bed.

"A lorry had run out of control into a shop window in Lyme Regis and I saw it happen," she recalls. Her mother, Peggy Perry, was the proof-reader during the 1950s in the days when Heber Bruce and Bill Harris were the editors.

"I rushed back to Bridport on the bus (no mobile phones in those days) and told mother who got a reporter to make enquiries and a few minutes later the presses were stopped. I was popular with the editor for getting a scoop over the Evening Echo but not with the printers who were hoping for an early evening"

Alison's mother was one of the first women union proof-readers in the county, maybe even the country.

Says Alison: "I remember some of the names from that time. Bob Borrowdale was the foreman and probably father of the chapel (shop steward), Charlie May, Cyril and Harry Little, Freddy Pike, Johnny Rice. Roger Bailey, Colin Hoath and Malcolm Clegg were the reporters.

Two theories as to why the Wip Wop nickname stuck

WHEN you think of newspapers and nicknames, the Thunderer comes instantly to mind. It's what the Times has been known as since 1830.

But the Bridport News also has its own nickname, which locals have been using for years.

There are two theories as to why the paper gained the alternative title, The Wip Wop.

One, rather unkindly, is that the stories were whipped out of the daily Echo newspaper and wopped into the Bridport News.

The other, more likely, version is that 'wip-wop, wip-wop' is the sound made by the old press in the days when the newspaper was printed at Frosts in West Street. And it appears there is even disagreement over how the Times got its nickname. Thomas Barnes's leading article on the Reform Bill, in which he called on the people to 'thunder for reform' is often cited as the nickname's origin.

But this was not published until January 1931 – almost a year after the Morning Herald called The Times 'The Great Earwigger of the Nation, otherwise The Leading Journal of Europe, otherwise The Awful Monosyllable, otherwise The Thunderer – but more commonly called The Blunderer'.

This stemmed from The Times's leader on a murky domestic drama involving the death in February 1830 of Lord Graves, Lord of the Bedchamber and Comptroller of the Household to HRH the Duke of Cumberland.

BIBLIOGRAPHY

The Bridport Railway, BL Jackson and MJ Tattershall,
The Oakwood Press 1979

Dorset Workhouses,
Dorset County Council 1980

The Cinemas of Bridport,
John Surry 1998

The Book of Bridport,
Basil Short and John Sales
Barracuda Books Limited 1980

ACKNOWLEDGEMENTS

I am indebted to Newsquest, the publishers of the Bridport News, for permission to scour the Bridport News archives and use the masthead

I would also like to thank Bridport Library for their help in using the microfilm reader; Bridport Museum and Mary Payne for photographs and the individual contributors, whose names feature in this book

PHOTOGRAPHS

(BM) Bridport Museum
(MH) Margery Hookings
(RB) Ron Boshier
(JG) John Gurd
(BN) Bridport News
(P and MP) Peter and Mary Payne
(DC) David Cozens
(CC) Chris Carson
(SH) Steve Hunt